NWA

E

TË

Longman
is an imprint of

PEARSON

y YORK
PRESS

YORK PRESS
322 Old Brompton Road, London SW5 9JH

PEARSON EDUCATION LIMITED
Edinburgh Gate, Harlow,
Essex CM20 2JE, United Kingdom

Associated companies, branches and representatives throughout the world

First published 1998
New edition 2004
This new and fully revised edition 2013

10 9 8 7 6 5 4 3 2 1

ISBN 978–1–4479–4883–4

Illustration on p. 9 by Neil Gower
Phototypeset by Chat Noir Design, France
Printed in Italy

Photo credits:

© David Lyons/Alamy for page 6 top / © Loop Images Ltd/Alamy for page 6 bottom / badahos/Shutterstock.com for page 7 / Claudio Baldini/Shutterstock.com for page 8 / Brenda Linskey/Shutterstock.com for page 10 / ©iStockphoto.com/Klubovy for page 11 / Pablo H Caridad/Shutterstock.com for page 12 / Zena Holloway/Shutterstock.com for page 13 / AJP/Shutterstock.com for page 14 / Rufous/Shutterstock.com for page 15 top / © Neil Barks/Alamy for page 15 bottom / © Jamie Robertson/Alamy for page 16 / bonzodog/Shutterstock.com for page 18 / Zena Holloway/Getty Images for page 19 / jordache/Shutterstock.com for page 20 / Subbotina Anna/Shutterstock.com for page 21 / jannoon028/Shutterstock.com for page 22 / Creative Travel Projects/Shutterstock.com for page 23 / Antonov Roman/Shutterstock.com for page 24 top / © book cover art Joana Kruse/Alamy for page 24 middle / debr22pics/Shutterstock.com for page 25 / Nastenok/Shutterstock.com for page 26 / kohy/Shutterstock.com for page 27 / CURAphotography/Shutterstock.com for page 28 / DenisNata/Shutterstock.com for page 29 / grintan/Shutterstock.com for page 30 / Kozlovskaya Ksenia/Shutterstock.com for page 31 / © ACE STOCK LIMITED/Alamy for page 32 / Valentina Photos/Shutterstock.com for page 33 middle / Danny Smythe/Shutterstock.com for page 34 top / CURAphotography/Shutterstock.com for page 34 bottom/ Aubord Dulac/Shutterstock.com for page 35 top / ©iStockphoto.com/ntripp for page 35 bottom / KellyNelson/Shutterstock.com for page 36 / Kevin Tracey/Shutterstock.com for page 37 / Artens/Shutterstock.com for page 38 / ©iStockphoto.com/motorenmano for page 39 middle / ollyy/Shutterstock.com for page 39 bottom / Olga Altunina/Shutterstock.com for page 40 / Tatiana Popova/Shutterstock.com for page 41 / katalinks/Shutterstock.com for page 42 / trabachar/Shutterstock.com for page 43 / Phase4Photography/Shutterstock.com for page 44 top / Chepko Danil Vitalevich/Shutterstock.com for page 44 bottom / Valeev/Shutterstock.com for page 45 / 1000 Words/Shutterstock.com for page 47 / Vasiliy Koval/Shutterstock.com for page 48 / 1000 Words/Shutterstock.com for page 49 / Rufous/Shutterstock.com for page 51 / caimacanul/Shutterstock.com for page 52 / conrado/Shutterstock.com for page 53 /©iStockphoto.com/setixela for page 54 top / Christian Mueller/Shutterstock.com for page 54 bottom / conrado/Shutterstock.com for page 55 / dcwcreations/Shutterstock.com for page 56 / Eduard Kyslynskyy/Shutterstock.com for page 57 / mihalec/Shutterstock.com for page 58 / Viktor Borovskikh/Shutterstock.com for page 60 / Kevin Day/Shutterstock.com for page 61 top / emin kuliyev/Shutterstock.com for page 61 middle / CURAphotography/Shutterstock.com for page 62 top / LilKar/Shutterstock.com for page 62 bottom / Annmarie Young/Shutterstock.com for page 63 / Vasiliy Koval/Shutterstock.com for page 64 / Ron Koeberer/Getty Images for page 65 middle / Veronika Trofer/Shutterstock.com for page 65 bottom / Zena Holloway/Getty Images for page 66 middle / bonzodog/Shutterstock.com for page 66 bottom / ©iStockphoto.com/THEPALMER for page 67 top / Simon Podgorsek/Getty Images for page 67 middle / Zena Holloway/Getty Image for page 67 bottom / ambrozinio/Shutterstock.com for page 69 top / Horiyan/Shutterstock.com for page 69 middle / My Good Images/Shutterstock.com for page 70 top / mosista/Shutterstock.com for page 70 bottom / Pavel Ignatov/Shutterstock.com for page 71 top / Natali Glado/Shutterstock.com for page 71 bottom / Shelli Jensen/Shutterstock.com for page 72 / Arogant/Shutterstock.com for page 73 / ©iStockphoto.com/RapidEye for page 74 top / ©iStockphoto.com/AnthiaCumming for page 74 bottom / Mariusz Szczygiel/Shutterstock.com for page 75 / robert_s/Shutterstock.com for page 76 / Willyam Bradberry/Shutterstock.com for page 77 / Ismael Jorda/Shutterstock.com for page 78 top / Ammentorp Photography/Shutterstock.com for page 78 middle / Matt Gibson/Shutterstock.com for page 79 / lynea/Shutterstock.com for page 80 / stocknshares/Shutterstock.com for page 81 / Baloncici/Shutterstock.com for page 82 top / tristan tan/Shutterstock.com for page 82 bottom / Kamira/Shutterstock.com for page 83 / ollyy/Shutterstock.com for page 84 top / Elenamiv/Shutterstock.com for page 84 bottom / Patrick Branwell Bronte/Getty Images for page 85 top / Shkanov Alexey/Shutterstock.com for page 85 bottom / Pavlo Loushkin for page 86 top / turtix/Shutterstock.com for page 86 bottom / © Q-Images/Alamy for page 87 / ©iStockphoto.com/Goldfaery for page 101 / ©iStockphoto.com/skynesher for page 103

CONTENTS

PART FIVE: CONTEXTS AND CRITICAL DEBATES

PART SIX: GRADE BOOSTER

ESSENTIAL STUDY TOOLS

PART ONE: INTRODUCING *JANE EYRE*

HOW TO STUDY *JANE EYRE*

These Notes can be used in a range of ways to help you read, study and (where relevant) revise for your exam or assessment.

READING THE NOVEL

Read the novel once, fairly quickly, for pleasure. This will give you a good sense of the over-arching shape of the **narrative**, and a good feel for the highs and lows of the action, the pace and tone, and the sequence in which information is withheld or revealed. You could ask yourself:

- How do individual characters change or develop? How do my own responses to them change?
- From whose point of view is the novel told? Does this change or remain the same?
- Are the events presented chronologically, or is the time scheme altered in some way?
- What impression do the locations and settings, such as Lowood and Thornfield, make on my reading and response to the text?
- What sort of language, style and form am I aware of as the novel progresses? Does Charlotte Brontë structure the novel precisely, or is there a more relaxed approach – or both? Does she use **imagery**, or recurring **motifs** and **symbols**?

On your second reading, make detailed notes around the key areas highlighted above and in the Assessment Objectives, such as form, language, structure (AO2), links and connections to other texts (AO3) and the context/background for the novel (AO4). These may seem quite demanding, but these Notes will suggest particular elements to explore or jot down.

INTERPRETING OR CRITIQUING THE NOVEL

Although it's not helpful to think in terms of the novel being 'good' or 'bad', you should consider the different ways the novel can be read. How have critics responded to it? Do their views match yours – or do you take a different viewpoint? Are there different ways you can interpret specific events, characters or settings? This is a key aspect in AO3, and it can be helpful to keep a log of your responses and the various perspectives which are expressed both by established critics, and also by classmates, your teacher, or other readers.

REFERENCES AND SOURCES

You will be expected to draw on critics' comments, or refer to source information from the period or the present. Make sure you make accurate, clear notes of writers or sources you have used, for example noting down titles of works, authors' names, website addresses, dates, etc. You may not have to reference all these things when you respond to a text, but knowing the source of your information will allow you to go back to it, if need be – and to check its accuracy and relevance.

REVISING FOR AND RESPONDING TO AN ASSESSED TASK OR EXAM QUESTION

The structure and the contents of these Notes are designed to help to give you the relevant information or ideas you need to answer tasks you have been set. First, identify the key words or ideas from the task (for example, 'form', 'language', 'Mr Rochester', etc.), then read the relevant parts of the Notes that relate to these terms or words, selecting what is useful for revision or your written response. Then, turn to **Part Six: Grade Booster** for help in formulating your response.

GRADE BOOSTER **AO2**

Finding good quotations to support your interpretation of the characters will greatly enhance and strengthen your points.

CHECK THE BOOK **AO1**

The York Handbook *Dictionary of Literary Terms*, by Martin Gray, provides explanations of the special vocabulary that will help you understand and write about novels like *Jane Eyre*.

JANE EYRE IN CONTEXT

CHARLOTTE BRONTË'S LIFE AND TIMES

1816 Charlotte Brontë is born on 21 April at Thornton, Yorkshire, third child of Patrick and Maria Brontë.

1817 Charlotte's brother Patrick Branwell born.

1820 Charlotte's sister Anne born. Charlotte's father Patrick Brontë becomes Perpetual Curate of Haworth. The family move to the village.

1821 Charlotte's mother dies.

1824 Charlotte, with her sisters Emily (b. 1818), Maria (b. 1813) and Elizabeth (b. 1815), sent to Clergy Daughters' School, Cowan Bridge.

1825 Maria dies on 6 May from tuberculosis. On 15 June Elizabeth dies from tuberculosis. Charlotte and Emily are removed from school.

1831 Charlotte goes to Miss Wooler's Roe Head School, near Huddersfield.

1832 Charlotte leaves Roe Head School, runs the household and teaches her sisters at home.

1835 Charlotte returns to Roe Head School as a teacher.

1837 Queen Victoria is crowned.

1838 Charlotte resigns from her job as a teacher.

1839 Charlotte joins the Sidgwick family as a governess. She refuses two proposals of marriage, both from clergymen.

1845 Charlotte begins work to get her and her sisters' work published under pseudonyms. She is 'Currer Bell'.

1847 *Jane Eyre* is published.

1854 Charlotte marries Arthur Bell Nicholls.

1855 Charlotte dies due to complications in early pregnancy.

JANE EYRE: A SHOCKING NOVEL?

Begun in 1846, *Jane Eyre* was initially published in October 1847 by Smith, Elder & Co. in three volumes under the supposed editorship of 'Currer Bell'. Charlotte and her sisters published under male-sounding pseudonyms because, as the Poet Laureate Robert Southey explained, when Charlotte sent him some of her poetry with a view to publication, 'Literature cannot be the business of a woman's life: and it ought not to be' (T. J. Wise & J. A. Symington (eds.), *The Brontës, their Lives, Friendships and Correspondence* (1933), Vol. 1, pp. 155–6). This was the prevailing attitude at the time.

Indeed, as soon as *Jane Eyre* was published, the novel attracted vehement criticism. This criticism emerged because of the novel's attack on **Evangelicalism** and, given its quite explicit portrayal of physical and emotional desires, because of its supposedly coarse morality. Moreover, the novel does not have a moral as such – Charlotte Brontë always resisted writing for a purpose. Instead it consists of a deep psychological insight into an individual's emotional and intellectual needs. This, and the fact that Jane is in part an advocate for women, made many early readers suspicious.

However, Jane does have to combine passion with duty before she can live happily ever after, and despite the criticism, the novel became immensely popular. A second edition appeared in January 1848, followed by a third in April of the same year. Charlotte Brontë's publishers wanted her to illustrate the third edition, but she refused because she felt that she lacked the necessary skill and also believed that most of her characters were physically unattractive. The final version to be published during Charlotte Brontë's lifetime was a one-volume edition in 1850.

SETTING

A FIVE-ACT DRAMA

The setting of the novel is very important to its structure, which falls into five parts. This structure works because the novel is set in five different locations: Gateshead, Lowood, Thornfield Hall, Morton/Marsh End/Moor House and Ferndean Manor. Each time Jane moves from one setting to another the **narrative** breaks to set the scene and stress that this setting will form a new stage in Jane's life. It is as if we are moving from one act to another in a five-act drama – an **analogy** the narrator uses herself in Chapter XI: 'A new chapter in a novel is something like a new scene in a play; and when I draw up the curtain this time, reader, you must fancy you see a room in the George Inn at Millcote' (p. 111). There are also two scenes in which Jane travels back to a previous location: one when she goes from Thornfield to Gateshead, to visit her aunt, and one when she goes from Moor House to Thornfield, when she searches for Rochester. These allow us to form contrasts between Jane's early and later life, and help to link the sections together, so that the novel coheres.

TONE

Each setting is dominated by a different tone. At Gateshead, for instance, the tone is passionate, superstitious and wild. This reflects the fact that the narrative is focused on a child at this point and shows us the more irrational elements in Jane's character. The tone at Lowood is cold, hard and constrained and reflects the limitations placed on young women by religious thought and social convention. At Thornfield the setting is personal and **symbolic**, for instance the house itself is identified with Rochester, and the narrative veers between the pacey and the restrained. We feel Jane's pulse quickening as she begins to fall in love with her master, but we are also given a sense of the way in which she is torn between passion and self-control. At Moor House the tone again becomes more stifling and oppressive as Jane slips back into a more conventional way of behaving, and begins to feel the limitations and pressure of St John's urge to self-sacrifice. However, when we finally reach Ferndean we move at last from fear and anticipation to delight. The novel therefore oscillates between the irrational – Gateshead and Thornfield – and the rational – Lowood and Moor House – reflecting the divisions within Jane herself, until resolution is achieved at Ferndean.

SEASONS AND NATURE

The seasons and nature are an important part of the depiction of Jane's character. When Jane leaves Gateshead for Lowood she is sent out, literally, into the cold. We know that the school is essentially repressive not only because of the behaviour of the teachers, but also because of the wintry setting – passion, indeed life, has been brought to a standstill. In contrast to this, when her relationship with Rochester begins, on her return to Thornfield Hall after having made her peace with the Reeds, it is early summer. The setting is beautiful and is suggestive of the Garden of Eden – semi-wild, old-fashioned flowers draw Jane's attention, as does Thornfield's place in the landscape as a whole. There are allusions to Keats – a nightingale sings – as well as Shakespeare's *A Midsummer Night's Dream*, a play in which lovers are constantly tricked, turned around and bewitched by fairies.

GRADE BOOSTER **AO2**

It is important to support your argument by referring to relevant quotations. But, do make sure that it is clear to your reader what you want to say about them, and what you think they mean.

KEY THEMES AND ISSUES

CHECK THE BOOK A04

For a consideration of the gendered aspects of the ways in which *Jane Eyre* was originally reviewed see N. D. Thompson *Reviewing Sex: Gender and the Reception of Victorian Novels* (1996).

It is easy to identify with Jane Eyre, for though the novel was written over a century and a half ago Jane expresses a young girl's longing for fulfilment, and fulfilment on her own terms – a concept very much at odds with the dictates of society in her own day. '"Wicked and cruel boy!"' she shouts at Master Reed in the first chapter, '"You are like a murderer – you are like a slave-driver – you are like the Roman emperors!"' (Chapter I, p. 13) And, "[d]id ever anybody see such a picture of passion!" (Chapter I, p. 14) her witnesses declare. Jane's fierce rebellion is a constant throughout the book, and though she appears to follow a customary path, she actually grows to maturity as a sensible and strong-willed woman whose aspirations confound convention. As Q. D. Leavis suggested, 'The theme has, very properly dictated the form, and the theme is an urgently felt personal one' (Introduction to *Jane Eyre*, Penguin Classics edition, 1966, p. 11).

THE SUPERNATURAL AND THE GOTHIC

The **Gothic** became fashionable in the eighteenth century as an antidote to **Neoclassicism** – the influence of classical, Greek and Roman, culture. As in *Jane Eyre*, the Gothic often uses **defamiliarisation** to create its effects: estrangement from what is ordinary and commonplace. *Jane Eyre* is full of dramatic contrasts, in which things that are usually mundane and unremarkable become uncanny. It is so packed with supernatural detail, coincidence and magic that it seems at times to be a fairy tale, even though it is built upon the foundations of everyday life. The **narrative** is forceful and vivid, and leaves a lasting impression of both anguish and delight. It is, however, carefully structured, controlled and coherent. It shows us how Charlotte Brontë sought to write not only about what she observed, but also what was hidden and unseen.

CHECK THE BOOK A04

For an important nineteenth-century assessment of Charlotte Brontë's life and re-assessment of her work see Mrs Gaskell's *The Life of Charlotte Brontë* (1857). Gaskell undertook extensive research on Charlotte Brontë, her family and social circle, and wrote with painstaking accuracy in defence of *Jane Eyre*. Because Gaskell was a popular novelist herself, this biography was and remains influential.

STUDY FOCUS: IS *JANE EYRE* A ROMANCE? A02

On one level, *Jane Eyre* is a romance, the story of two people falling in love and defying convention to be together. But this is also a story of self-discovery. As we follow Jane, she grows and learns about the world around her – and learns more than mere books or schooling could teach her. In the process we experience her sincerity, her powerful feelings for Rochester and the intensity of their relationship.

We see that ultimately Jane chooses Rochester over St John because she comes to know herself and learns that the conventions of her day are simple habits of thought, not moral certainties. The sympathy that grows between Jane and Rochester is therefore much more than 'love', it is a sympathy of 'fellow-feeling; mutual sensibility; the quality of being affected by the affections [feelings] of another' as defined by Samuel Johnson in his *Dictionary* of 1755. In this respect Charlotte Brontë was influenced by the school of emotional moral philosophy, whose followers believed that the emotions – or feelings, as experienced through the sympathetic imagination – are meant to give us an innate sense of morality or to show us how our actions affect others.

CHARACTERS IN *JANE EYRE*

The Reeds

Mrs Reed ✗ m. **Mr Reed** ✗

Mrs Reed
Jane's cruel aunt (by marriage) who sends her to Lowood

Gateshead Hall

The Eyres

Mrs Eyre ✗ m. **Mr Eyre** ✗

Mrs Eyre
Jane's mother

Mr Eyre
Jane's father

Mr John Eyre
Jane's uncle who leaves her £20,000 in his will

The Rivers

Mrs Rivers ✗ m. **Mr Rivers** ✗

Moor House

Master John **Georgiana** **Eliza**

Jane's cousins

Miss Abbot
Nursemaid

Bessie
Nursemaid

St John
Minister at Morton. Proposes to Jane, but she declines

Mary **Diana**
Jane's cousins

Jane Eyre
Orphaned and has an unhappy childhood. Works for Mr Rochester. She runs away upon hearing about Bertha. Her cousin, St John asks her to marry him. She refuses and returns to Mr Rochester

Rosamund Oliver — Ⓜ — **Mr Granby**

Rich woman who hopes to marry St John, but he does not propose to her and she marries Mr Granby

Lowood School

Mr Brocklehurst
Headmaster

Miss Temple
Jane's teacher and friend

Helen Burns
Jane's friend

Mrs Fairfax
Housekeeper at Thornfield. Distant relative of Mr Rochester

Blanche Ingram
Hopes to marry Mr Rochester for his money

Ⓜ

Mr Rochester
Falls in love with Jane and tries to marry her, despite already being married. Injured in the fire started by Bertha

Celine Varens
Mr Rochester's ex-mistress and Adèle's mother

Bertha Mason
The first wife of Mr Rochester

Mr Mason
Bertha's brother. Works for Jane's uncle

Grace Poole
Maid at Thornfield. Cares for Bertha

Mr Briggs
Mr Mason's solicitor

Sophie
Adèle's French nurse

Adèle Varens
Looked after by Mr Rochester, taught by Jane

Thornfield Hall

KEY

——— Familial relationship

········· Other relationship

✗ Deceased

Ⓜ Married at the end of the novel

SYNOPSIS

CHILDHOOD AT GATESHEAD

At the beginning of the novel Jane Eyre is an orphan who lives with her well-to-do aunt, Mrs Reed, and cousins, Eliza, John and Georgiana. Jane is constantly bullied by her cousins, and her aunt always assumes that she is the guilty party whenever there is an argument. On one occasion Mrs Reed locks Jane in a room that is reputedly haunted, as punishment for a crime that she did not commit. Jane's nerves are shattered and the servants' apothecary is called in. Immeasurably unhappy, Jane is deeply relieved to discover that he has recommended she be sent away to boarding school. Before she leaves she makes friends with Bessie, the nursemaid who 'had a remarkable knack of narrative' (Chapter IV, p. 36), and wins a psychological battle against her aunt.

EDUCATION AT LOWOOD

Jane is sent to Lowood, a school for clergymen's daughters, where she makes friends with another pupil, Helen Burns, and the mistress, Miss Temple. Helen, who is deeply religious, gentle and forbearing, teaches Jane the value of self-control. However, the conditions at the school are appalling and, when the girls become sick, Helen dies of consumption. As a result, the school is reformed and in the end Jane stays on for a total of eight years, as pupil, then as assistant teacher. When Miss Temple leaves to marry, Jane begins to find life at the school restrictive and advertises for a new job.

EMPLOYMENT AT THORNFIELD

Jane is soon offered a place by a Mrs Fairfax as governess to 'a little girl, under ten years of age' (Chapter X, p. 105) at double her Lowood salary, and sets out to take up her new position as quickly as she can. When she arrives at Thornfield Hall she finds that Mrs Fairfax is housekeeper to the master, Edward Fairfax Rochester, and that the little girl, Adèle Varens, is his ward. The place suits Jane and she settles in quickly, but for some time does not see Rochester. She finally meets him as he rides towards Thornfield when she is out on an errand one day. His horse slips on some ice and he is obliged to seek her aid.

COURTSHIP AT THORNFIELD

As they become better acquainted Jane begins to feel drawn to Rochester; he is equally attracted by her intelligence and wit. While she is away from the hall visiting her dying aunt she misses him and he tries to make her jealous by pretending that he is going to marry a local heiress, Miss Blanche Ingram. Despite the differences in their station and age, Rochester finally proposes and Jane accepts. The match is ill-omened, however, and their wedding is interrupted by the arrival of Mr Richard Mason who declares that Rochester is already married to his sister, Bertha Mason. It becomes clear that there is indeed a Mrs Rochester, but that she is unstable and is kept under lock and key in the attic of Thornfield. Rochester pleads for Jane to go abroad with him as his mistress, to become '**Mrs Rochester – both virtually and nominally**' (Chapter XXVII, p. 350), but she cannot bring herself to stay and slips away from the hall before anyone can stop her.

LIFE WITH THE RIVERS FAMILY

Jane wanders destitute for some days. No one will help her or give her work until she is finally taken in by a clergyman, St John Rivers, and his sisters, Diana and Mary, who find Jane half-starved at their door. As she recovers from her ordeal she makes friends with the sisters and St John offers her a job as the village schoolmistress. She works at the school under the assumed name of Jane Elliott, but St John discovers her real name on one of her drawings. Through this he is eventually able to tell her that she is related to him and his sisters and that she has inherited a fortune from her uncle. She insists on sharing the money equally with her new-found family and hopes to be treated as their sister.

St John is a cold, ambitious man, who, though patient, is forbearing and exacting. He hopes to become a missionary and, in the end, asks Jane to marry him and travel to India as his help-mate. Jane says that though she might help him in his missionary work she cannot marry him because he does not love her. As he presses her on the matter and she begins to give way, she hears Rochester calling to her. Jane decides that she must find out what has become of Rochester before she can do anything else and travels back to Thornfield.

MARRIAGE TO ROCHESTER

When she reaches Thornfield Jane discovers that the house has been razed to the ground and further investigation reveals that the hall has been burnt down by Mrs Rochester. Edward Rochester is alive, but, in the process of trying to save his wife, has suffered terrible injuries. Jane determines to find him and, though he is maimed and blind, they finally marry. The novel closes with an account of their married life, including the partial return of Rochester's sight and the birth of their son, and a brief summary of what has happened to the Rivers family.

CHAPTER I

SUMMARY

- We are introduced to Jane's relatives, her widowed aunt Mrs Reed, and her cousins Master John Reed and his sisters Eliza and Georgina, and also to the two servants, the nursemaid Bessie and Mrs Reed's servant Abbot.
- Jane Eyre has not been allowed to sit with her aunt and cousins after dinner – she is reading Bewick's *History of British Birds* (1797, 1804).
- Master John mistreats Jane. She is injured and Jane and Master John get into a fight. When Aunt Reed is called, Jane, bleeding, is sent to 'the red-room' (p. 14).

ANALYSIS

A CHILD'S POINT OF VIEW

This chapter is one of the earliest accounts given by a child from a child's point of view in English fiction. Though it is actually being **narrated** in retrospect by the mature Jane Rochester several years after the close of Chapter XXXVII, it nonetheless provides us with a highly suggestive portrait of Jane Eyre's thoughts and feelings as a child.

STUDY FOCUS: VISUAL CONTRASTS **A02**

In the 'Folds of scarlet drapery' and the 'drear November day' (p. 10) we find an early example of the kind of visual contrast that is characteristic of the novel. The references to Bewick help disclose Jane's state of mind. The book is full of **sublime** – powerful and **Romantic** – **images** of shipwrecks, storms, Arctic wastes, high mountain reaches, death and disaster. However, Master Reed owns the books and the 'bookshelves' or, as he says, 'will do in a few years' (p. 13), which therefore work **symbolically** to suggest that even though a girl may understand what's written, conventionally it is the boy who will grow up to be the legitimate heir in control of the household's documents, wills and

deeds, regardless of his learning or nature. Moreover, her inferior position within the Reed family is made brutally clear through her fight with John. Written authority is backed up in his case by physical and verbal violence, so that he literally 'throws the book' at Jane. Property ownership, Charlotte Brontë suggests, is manifestly masculine. Master Reed rules by might and right. Despite his position of power, John meets an unfortunate end. To what extent is this **foreshadowed** by his introduction here?

CHECK THE BOOK **A03**

Edmund Burke, in his *A Philosophical Enquiry into the Origin of our Ideas of the Sublime and the Beautiful* (1757) argued that sublime objects are awe inspiring and vast, but also evoke dread. The sublime was a key element of Romantic writing, and the Romantics saw it as something that could not be processed by the rational mind, but which evoked sensations that were close to a religious experience.

GLOSSARY

10	**Where the Northern ... Hebrides**	from James Thomson, *The Seasons* (1726–30)
11	**'Pamela'**	novel by Samuel Richardson (1740)
11	**'Henry, Earl of Moreland'**	John Wesley's abridgement of Henry Brooke, *The Fool of Quality* (1781)
13	**Goldsmith's 'History of Rome'**	Oliver Goldsmith's abridgement of *The Roman History* (1772)

CHAPTER II

SUMMARY

- Miss Abbot and Bessie lock Jane in the 'red-room' (p. 16).
- Jane becomes frightened. She thinks that the room is haunted and that her uncle, Mr Reed, who died in the room is about to come for her.
- Jane screams in terror. Miss Abbot and Bessie come to see what is wrong.
- Jane's aunt leaves her in the room for another hour. Jane passes out.

ANALYSIS

PASSIONATE JANE

In this chapter the supernatural mixes with mundane detail about the Reeds and Jane's origin and background. She is just ten and her fear of the 'red-room' (p. 16), connected as it is with death, seems quite natural. In addition to the child's point of view, however, we are also given a privileged insight into her position by the adult Jane who looks back and reflects on the scene.

The fact that Jane is described as 'a mad cat' (p. 15) and is made to sit fixedly on a chair as part of her punishment **foreshadows** Mrs Rochester whom we first meet in Chapter XXV. We also learn that Jane can be quite superstitious as well as passionate, and she battles with both tendencies throughout the course of the novel.

STUDY FOCUS: THE RED-ROOM `A02`

This chapter can be read symbolically as Jane's transition from girlhood into the early stages of womanhood. Jane's experiences at Gateshead represent a typically Victorian education in which a passionate girl is taught how to become a passive and restrained woman. In Charlotte Brontë's work the colour red, which connotes fire, is normally associated with sexuality – white and coldness with its absence. Jane being made to sit in the red-room is therefore indicative of her entry into adolescence. Through this experience Jane also learns that she will be subject to unjust and oppressive punishments and that she cannot retreat into childhood any more – she cannot go back to the nursery. It is only once she faints, in others words, submits fully to her circumstances, that she is taken out of the room. We should consider to what extent she is treated as a delicate creature, as the Victorians considered a good woman should be, after this.

> **CONTEXT** `A04`
>
> Jane's superstition suggests a metaphysical philosophy. In other words, Jane's world view includes the immaterial and the abstract; she believes that there is something beyond or independent of the human.

GLOSSARY

16	**'cover'**	deceitfulness
17	**Marseilles**	stiff cotton fabric

EXTENDED COMMENTARY

CHAPTER II, PP. 16–18

From 'The red-room was a spare chamber' to 'I quailed to the dismal present.'

This passage comes from early on in *Jane Eyre* and contains the vivid episode where Jane is trapped in the red-room as punishment by her relatives.

The Gateshead section of the novel is dominated by a sense of passion, sensuality and superstition, reflecting both Jane's age – she is just ten at this point – and the more irrational side of her character. The self-indulgent Mrs Reed dominates the house, her children are spoilt and Jane learns to become as headstrong as the rest of them. In the red-room she begins to discover that there is a down-side to letting her emotions get the better of her, but at this point she is still enjoying the pleasant after-glow of rebellion. Her natural unease at being in her dead uncle's room is, however, gradually being intensified by her superstition and overexcited state of mind.

The tone is initially as heavy as the stately furniture, while the silence and abandonment of the room is suggested by words like 'subdued', 'muffled', 'vacant'; even the dust is 'quiet' (p. 17). We see the room from Jane's nervous point of view and she sees the objects within it quite unnaturally. The bed is not simply a bed but becomes a 'tabernacle', the chair beside it becomes 'a pale throne' (p. 17), she herself becomes 'a real spirit', 'one of those tiny phantoms, half fairy, half imp' (p. 18). Each object metamorphoses into something that is alien and frightening and though the scene is described quite tersely, **journalistically**, it is also highly suggestive.

The way of seeing described in this passage stays with Jane throughout the novel. Whenever she is unable to explain an experience or other phenomenon she looks for a supernatural or unnatural origin. As she matures and learns about the emotion, experience or object in more detail, she begins to assign to it a rational explanation. Shortly after this passage ends, for instance, she says that she wondered as a child why she merited such bad treatment from the Reeds; as an adult she is able to reflect on this and explain that it was because she was so unlike them. We are therefore drawn into sympathy for Jane as she sits alone and frightened in a haunted room, but we also gain a more mature understanding of the way in which she has brought much of her ill-treatment upon herself. The point at which she looks into the mirror crystallises one such moment of balanced perception.

CONTEXT **A04**

At this point in time, it was legal for a single woman to control property if she had inherited it, as Jane Eyre does later in the story. But, until the Married Women's Property Act of 1870 a woman who married gave up her property and earnings to her husband. A married woman did not have the same property rights as a single woman until the Married Women's Property Act of 1884. Widows like Mrs Reed would only hold their deceased husband's inherited property until their eldest son came of age.

The mirror in which she sees herself as a phantom and the punishment of sitting on a chair in a locked and abandoned room for a fit of passion also form a link between Jane and Mrs Rochester, who is also described as a kind of phantom. The redness of the room itself is **symbolic** of passion and unreason, and of course it houses restricted and confidential documents – the symbols of Mrs Reed's property and wealth inherited from her husband – just like the attic at Thornfield Hall. This prefigures the link that is established between Jane and Bertha when Jane wanders, daydreaming on the third storey at Thornfield – 'if there were a ghost at Thornfield Hall, this would be its haunt' (Chapter XI, p. 125) – and suggests that if she had not learnt to control her irrational instincts and had stayed with Edward Rochester after Bertha's existence is revealed, then she would have also have become, if not actually mentally ill, then as powerless and lacking in the ability to control her own life as Bertha is.

CONTEXT **A03**

Eighteenth-century **Gothic** novels were usually set in the past, often in Southern European Catholic countries, and featured spectacular landscapes, castles and monasteries, as well as fantastical and eerie goings on. By the nineteenth century, Gothic writing had become more domestic. Though still suspenseful and supernatural, Gothic novels were generally given English, often urban, settings and focused on the home.

CHAPTER III

SUMMARY

CONTEXT **A04**

The Apothecaries Act of 1815 regulated the provision of medicine and medical advice, but there was a conflict between the physicians and the apothecaries about who should dispense medicine and who should provide medical treatment. Apothecaries were cheaper than physicians and not supposed to be paid for medical treatment. They often acted as a kind of early General Practitioner at this time.

- Jane wakes up to find that the servants' apothecary, Mr Lloyd, has been called to look at her.
- Bessie tries to cheer her up, but Jane can be tempted by neither food nor books.
- Mr Lloyd asks her if she would like to leave.
- Jane says that though she would not like to go to her father's family – whom she assumes are poor – she would like to go to school.

ANALYSIS

JANE: THE 'POOR ORPHAN CHILD'

Bessie's traditional ballad reflects Jane's condition as a 'poor orphan child' (p. 27) and we also find out more about Jane's mother here. Bessie's retelling of a story about a 'great black dog' (p. 24) is picked up in Chapter XII, and the idea that all the fairies have left England is reiterated in Chapter XIII. We can therefore begin to guess that Bessie is very important to Jane. The nursemaid does in fact seem to care for Miss Eyre after all, and this sets the tone for their reconciliation in Chapter IV. However, Jane's unconventional appearance not simply her outlandish behaviour will clearly remain a problem, given the other servant, Abbot's opinion that she could be pitied 'if she were a nice, pretty child' (p. 31). Even Bessie allows that 'a beauty like Miss Georgiana would be more moving in the same condition' (p. 31). Successful femininity clearly requires good looks.

STUDY FOCUS: JANE'S SNOBBERY **A02**

Because we only ever receive information from Jane's point of view and because we get to know her deepest thoughts and feelings, we tend to assume that she is a reliable **narrator**. However, she is not always a sympathetic character. She is a precocious girl and there are moments when the reader feels quite sorry for Mrs Reed. Jane's initial response to the plight of the poor serves to remind us that she is still just a child, brought up by the lazy and snobbish Reeds. She also maintains some of this attitude as seen in her later treatment of the Rivers's servant in Chapter XXIX. She uses the word 'caste' (p. 30) (see **Empire** in **Part Five: Contexts and critical debates**) rather than 'class', and it therefore seems Jane sees the social divide as insurmountable and the idea of crossing it quite taboo.

GLOSSARY

25	**I ought to forgive … did**	reference to Luke 23:34
25	**'Gulliver's Travels'**	satire by Jonathan Swift (1726)
26	**'In the days … ago'**	popular song, Edward Ransford (c.1840)
27	**'My feet … orphan child'**	unknown ballad
30	**backboards**	devices meant to improve the way you sit or stand

CHAPTER IV

SUMMARY

- It is decided that Jane shall go to school.
- Jane continues to stand up for herself and starts to talk back to her aunt, who tells her cousins to stay away from her.
- Jane finally meets her future headmaster, Mr Brocklehurst, **'a black pillar! … straight, narrow, sable-clad'** (p. 38).
- Deeply upset when her aunt sullies her reputation, Jane tells Mrs Reed what she thinks of her.
- Mrs Reed is frightened and Jane exults in her first real victory over her aunt.
- Bessie likes the girl's new-found self-confidence, and Jane and Bessie make friends again.

ANALYSIS

LINKS ACROSS THE NOVEL

We are never surprised by Jane's behaviour as we move through the novel because the foundation is laid for every action and response. Jane's dislike of the company who turn up for Christmas prefigures her uneasiness at the arrival of guests at Thornfield in Chapter XVII. Though Jane swears never to call Mrs Reed 'aunt' again, when she does so, in Chapter XXI, she is quite self-conscious about it. We see all the characters in the novel from Jane's point of view and a perfect example of this can be found in the way our opinion of Bessie changes as Jane begins to see her differently.

STUDY FOCUS: BROCKLEHURST — A02

Mr Brocklehurst is described by Jane as if he were the big bad wolf from 'Little Red Riding Hood': **'what a great nose! and what a mouth! and what large prominent teeth!'** (p. 39). This reflects the influence of Bessie's stories on Jane and the child's point of view, but the implication is also that Mr Brocklehurst is a liar so when he says Mrs Reed is **'judicious'** (p. 41) and that he is consistent we should not believe him. Jane's replies to his questions about the Bible, heaven and hell are supposed to imply criticism of his highly conventional theology. However, they might also suggest that Jane has not read the Gospels, which would have taught her to forgive those who harm her, as Helen Burns points out in Chapter VI.

GLOSSARY

33	**waited**	awaited
33	**stirred my corruption**	(Christian) made me angry
35	**graven image**	(biblical) idol
36	**traffic**	trade
40	**to take … flesh**	Ezekiel, 11;19 and 36:26; 2 Corinthians 3:3, 6
42	**"Child's Guide"**	based on a monthly religious pamphlet, *The Children's Friend*
46	**'onding on snaw'**	'pelting with snow', from Walter Scott, *The Heart of Midlothian*

GRADE BOOSTER — A02

Bessie tells Jane that she **'should be bolder'** (p. 47), which is striking as Jane's behaviour is often quite **melodramatic**. Think about the characters that most influence Jane during the course of the novel.

CHECK THE BOOK — A03

This chapter draws on the sorts of nursery or fairy stories – 'Cinderella' and 'Little Red Riding Hood' – that Bessie tells Jane. For an interesting comparative selection of fairy tales from around the world see *The Virago Book of Fairy Tales* (1990) and *The Second Book of Virago Fairy Tales* (1992) both edited by Angela Carter. Angela Carter was well-known for reworking fairy tales like these in her own work, e.g. *The Bloody Chamber* (1979) and *The Magic Toyshop* (1981).

CHAPTER V

SUMMARY

- Jane leaves Gateshead on 19 January.
- She arrives at Lowood school in the dark, rain and wind. She is so tired and overexcited that she cannot eat any supper.
- At breakfast the next morning the porridge is too burnt to eat. To the girls' surprise the headmistress, Miss Temple, decides to serve the girls lunch.
- During her first day Jane meets Burns, another pupil, who tells her about the school, its principles and its teachers.

ANALYSIS

EXPOSITION AND INFORMATION

This chapter sets the scene for the Lowood section of the book and the next stage in Jane's life. It is therefore largely **expository**; much of the information is provided by the dialogue that takes place between Jane and the other pupil – Helen Burns. The harsh regime at the school is indicated by the cold weather, and its exacting nature by the school's garden. Though the garden is wide, it is enclosed by high walls and a large number of 'little beds … assigned as gardens for the pupils to cultivate' (p. 58). This is based on the Victorian idea that through gardening children might themselves become cultivated, i.e. good and moral, but also suggests that at Lowood it is believed that nature should and will be tamed. This becomes explicit in Chapter VII. Burns's character is suggested by her choice of reading matter: *Rasselas*.

STUDY FOCUS: MISS TEMPLE   A01

In this chapter we discover that the schoolmistress's last name is Miss Maria Temple. 'Temple' indicates her devout nature, and her first name, 'Maria', is derived from Mary, the name of Christ's mother. Maria was also Charlotte Brontë's eldest sister's name. It is clear that Miss Temple will become a dearly loved figure and an important role model for Jane. How significant are names generally in *Jane Eyre*?

KEY QUOTATION: CHAPTER V

'[T]he door opened, and an individual carrying a light entered; … a tall lady with dark hair, dark eyes, and a pale and large forehead; her figure was partly enveloped in a shawl, her countenance was grave, her bearing erect.' (p. 52)

Possible interpretations:

- Though unnamed, the individual described in the quotation is Miss Temple. The description of her 'bearing' and 'countenance' links Miss Temple to the figure of Christ.
- The **imagery** draws on the Victorian association of Christ and the Church with light, and the door might be interpreted as the door to the soul.
- Charlotte Brontë's description of Miss Temple here and elsewhere in Chapter V draws on **physiognomy**.

CHAPTER VI

SUMMARY

- Jane is enrolled as a member of the fourth class and begins her lessons.
- She sees her new friend, Burns, participating in a history lesson.
- The teacher, Miss Scatcherd, seems to be particularly cruel to Burns. For instance, though the water was frozen so that no one could wash that morning, Miss Scatcherd says to Burns: 'You dirty, disagreeable girl! you have never cleaned your nails this morning!' (p. 64).
- Burns is flogged, but takes it stoically.
- In the evening, Jane speaks to Burns and finds out that her first name is Helen.
- Helen Burns explains the principles of endurance, duty and self-sacrifice to Jane, as based on the New Testament Gospels.

ANALYSIS

HELEN BURNS

The chapter largely consists of the conversation that takes place between Jane and Helen Burns. Though this dialogue covers some complex theological ground, it is nonetheless quite naturalistic and provides us with a deep insight into Helen's character. Helen offers one solution to Jane's problem – the need to quell her passionate nature – and Jane does learn from her, as we begin to see in the following chapters. But Helen's faith is also essentially inward-looking – indicated by her tendency to slip into a dream-like state – and she looks forward to death: 'I live in calm, looking to the end' (p. 70).

STUDY FOCUS: A COLD WORLD — A03

Jane has been sent out from Gateshead, literally, into the cold. We know that the school is essentially repressive not only because of the behaviour of the teachers, but also because of the wintry setting – passion, indeed life, has been brought to a standstill. As we saw in the previous chapter, the gardens may contain flowers in the future – the girls may grow up to be pretty young women – but for the moment they have been frozen solid. A psychological reading would associate this with the endless waste of adolescence, as is also suggested by Jane's comment in the next chapter that she is having an 'irksome' time struggling 'with difficulties in habituating myself to new rules and unwonted tasks' (Chapter VII, p. 71). Notice how the miserly way in which the school is run is not only indicated through the girls' food, but also the use of rushlights (an inexpensive candle made by soaking part of a rush plant in grease).

REVISION FOCUS: TASK 1 — A04

Consider the following:

- The importance of religion in *Jane Eyre*.
- The role of property and class in *Jane Eyre*.

Write opening paragraphs for essays based on these discussion points. Set out your arguments clearly and ensure that your paragraphs link to each other in a logical way.

CRITICAL VIEWPOINT — A02

Even the minor character's names often reflect their temperament and interests. For example, 'Miss Temple' is quite saintly compared to the harsh 'Miss Scatcherd' who has a name that is evocative of scratches and shards.

CONTEXT — A03

Stoicism includes the idea that life is best lived without the more extreme or violent feelings and that the best way to achieve such freedom is through virtuous living. This philosophy is derived from several Classical Greek thinkers.

CHAPTER VII

SUMMARY

- It is winter and all the girls suffer from the cold and hunger. The older girls sit in front of the fire and take most of the younger girls' food.

- The proprietor, Mr Brocklehurst, visits the school.

- Brocklehurst criticises Miss Temple for giving the girls lunch, picks on one of the girls, Julia Severn, for having naturally curly hair, and makes Jane sit in front of the whole school while he calls her a liar.

ANALYSIS

CONTRASTS

Jane's conflict with Mr Brocklehurst was **foreshadowed** in Chapter IV. Jane is falsely accused (as she was in Chapter I) and begins to panic (as she did in Chapter II) but by this point, thanks to Helen Burns's help and Miss Temple's example, Jane proves that she can control her emotions and take her punishment. Mr Brocklehurst never lives up to his Evangelical principles and his character is formed in direct opposition to that of the other clergyman in the novel, St John Rivers, whom we meet in Chapter XXVIII. Brocklehurst is described (in Chapter VII) as a 'black column' (p. 73), whereas St John is 'marble' (Chapter XXXV, p. 473); Brocklehurst is a hypocrite, unlike St John who is ruthlessly consistent and as 'inexorable as death' (Chapter XXXI, p. 421).

STUDY FOCUS: BROCKLEHURST'S INCONSISTENCY A02

Brocklehurst's inconsistency is made clear in his attack on Julia Severn and the entrance of his fashionably dressed wife and daughters. Brocklehurst's religious worldview becomes abundantly clear when he insists that the girls must neither 'conform to the world' nor 'to nature' (p. 76). His principles are impossible to live up to. Moreover, though he looks to a higher state of being in 'Grace', i.e. at one with God, his way of bringing this about is to maim God's creation: cut off Julia's natural curls. It seems to be implied that Lowood is the worst of all Christian worlds.

GLOSSARY

72	**starved**	frozen
73	**'Coming Man'**	man likely to achieve eminence, but also the expectation that Christ will return – the Second Coming
75	**take up their cross**	Mark 8:34
75	**man shall not live by bread alone ... God**	Matthew 4:4
76	**Grace**	idea that God will redeem certain individuals and not others
76	**cup and platter**	Matthew 13:25–6
77	**false front**	hairpiece
79	**'Brahma and kneels before Juggernaut'**	suggests that Jane prays to the Hindu god Krishna; foreshadows St John Rivers's attempts to take her as a missionary to India

---

CONTEXT A04

Brocklehurst is one of many **Evangelicals** represented negatively in nineteenth-century fiction. Others include Mr Murdstone in Charles Dickens's *David Copperfield* and Mr Slope in Anthony Trollope's *Barchester Towers*.

CRITICAL VIEWPOINT A02

The older girls standing closer to the fire than the younger ones can be see as **symbolising** the fact that the older girls are that bit closer to sexual maturity. Eva Figes – a feminist critic who develops a psychological interpretation of the novel – has pointed out that the incident when Brocklehurst demands that Julia Severn has her hair cut can be read as an instance of the repression and denial of excess female sexuality. In a psychological reading, the frozen world of Lowood equates to the containment or repression of the emerging, threatening energies of sexual maturity.

CHAPTER VIII

SUMMARY

- School is dismissed. Jane is left alone and breaks down in tears. Her friend Helen comforts her.
- Miss Temple takes Helen and Jane to her room and takes them under her wing for the evening.
- Jane is awed by Helen's knowledge. When Helen reads from Virgil Jane finds her 'organ of veneration expanding at every sounding line' (p. 87).
- Jane tells her story to Miss Temple, who writes to Mr Lloyd, the apothecary, for corroboration. When he writes back, she gets the whole school together and publicly clears Jane's reputation.
- Jane is promoted to a higher class and goes on to learn French and drawing.

ANALYSIS

PHRENOLOGICAL DESCRIPTIONS

In this chapter we can see the influence of phrenology on Charlotte Brontë's writing. Based on the idea that certain areas of the brain have particular functions, phrenology involved the measurement of the skull in order to assess the shape and size of these individual areas or organs. These measurements were then supposed to give indications of a person's character and likely behaviour. For example, the 'organ of individuality' was believed to be in the middle of the lower part of the forehead. A person with a well-developed organ of individuality would be a close observer of material details and have a great aptitude for natural history. The 'organ of veneration', which Jane feels is expanded by Helen's abilities, was connected with religious worship, but also an individual's inclination to look up to their superiors and to be charitable.

STUDY FOCUS: HELEN THE ROLE MODEL   **A02**

Helen's conversation with Jane shows that self-reliance can come from faith; self-respect and individuality are stressed here above all else. The fact that Jane takes some of this teaching on board becomes clear in her visit to Gateshead and flight from Thornfield later on in the novel. When Jane tells her story to Miss Temple we can see that she has already learnt to control some of her worst excesses thanks to Helen. And she finds that she can accommodate the privations of Lowood with the help of her new friends. Helen exemplifies the Christian ideal of turning one's cheek, forgiving one's enemies and meek endurance. She is a model of morality and of learning, but Jane is doubtful about the validity of Helen's example: 'in the tranquillity she imparted there was an alloy of inexpressible sadness' (p. 83). Helen's faith makes her turn away from life and her subsequent illness and death is **foreshadowed** several times – Jane even notices her in the garden for the first time (Chapter V) because she coughs. Consider how important Helen is for Jane.

CONTEXT   **A03**

Charlotte Brontë and her sisters – like many radical (and Christian) middle-class intellectuals such as the social commentator Harriet Martineau (1802–76) – subscribed to phrenology. George Combe's *Elements of Phrenology* (1834) helped promote the pseudoscience in the UK. In its later forms phrenology became closely associated with anthropology and definitions of racial 'type', but at this point was more closely associated with issues of social reform, education and crime.

GLOSSARY

87	**phylactery** Jewish, small box holding scripture extracts worn on the body
88	*Etre* the infinitive of the French verb 'to be'
88	**Barmecide supper** fantasy feast
88	**Cuyp-like** after the seventeenth-century Dutch landscape painter Albert Cuyp

CHAPTER IX

SUMMARY

- As winter gives way to spring, so forty-five out of the eighty pupils fall ill from typhus.
- Some of the girls are taken away by relatives, the teachers nurse the others and the well ones are left to look after themselves. Many of the girls die.
- Jane remains fairly well and can play in the spring sunshine, but Helen becomes very sick from consumption.
- One evening Jane slips in to visit Helen, determined to see her friend before she dies. They talk a little and Jane is amazed by Helen's faith.
- Helen asks Jane to stay with her and while Jane sleeps, Helen dies.

ANALYSIS

'READER'

In this chapter we see the first direct reference to the reader: 'True, reader' (p. 93). This is a device which recurs several times throughout the remainder of the novel, the last being 'Reader, I married him.' (Chapter XXXVIII, p. 517). This device creates a close bond between the **narrator** and the reader and draws the latter into the story. These petitions to the reader always come at moments of heightened intensity or action, often adding detail to a relationship or Jane's thoughts at that moment. In this case it acts as a supplement to the narrative, and highlights just how important Helen Burns is to Jane.

HELEN BURNS DIES

The final conversation between Jane and Helen is convincing and naturalistic and there is considerable **pathos** in Helen's death. In the morning Jane is merely sleeping while Helen is starkly '– dead' (p. 98). Death and sickness are contrasted very sharply in this chapter with health and the will to live, both in the girls' environment and in their beliefs.

CONTEXT **A04**

Jane says typhus 'breathed' (p. 91) through Lowood. At this time disease was often supposed to be spread by bad air, called 'miasma'. One of the leading medical practitioners of the day therefore declared: 'All smell is, if it be intense, immediate acute disease; and eventually we may say that, by depressing the system and rendering it susceptible to the action of other causes, all smell is disease.' (Edwin Chadwick, 1846)

STUDY FOCUS: ALTER EGOS **A02**

We can see Helen Burns as Jane's alter ego – following the association of 'Burns' with fire and passion, Helen can be seen as that side of Jane that she must learn to repress in order to survive in Victorian society. Helen has survived in the hostile, frigid world of Lowood by going inside herself – by daydreaming – but this is not enough and she is burned up (by fever). Helen is Jane's alter ego here because she dies just as Jane begins to control her feelings, and once Helen dies Jane is much more easily schooled. It is only as an adult, married woman that Jane can resurrect this part of herself, as we might see from the final few lines of the chapter: 'Her [Helen's] grave … for fifteen years … was only covered by a grassy mound; but now a gray [sic] marble tablet marks the spot, inscribed with her name, and the word "*Resurgam*"' (p. 98).

GLOSSARY

96	**'long home'**	death
98	**'Resurgam'**	(Latin) 'I shall rise again'

CHAPTER X

SUMMARY

- The outbreak of typhus leads to an enquiry into the running of Lowood and the school is reformed.
- Jane stays a further eight years, six as a pupil and two as an assistant teacher.
- Miss Temple leaves, in order to marry a clergyman. Jane then realises that it is time to go out into the world.
- Jane advertises for a new post and receives a letter from a Mrs Fairfax of Thornfield offering her a situation looking after a girl at £30 a year, double her Lowood salary.
- Jane obtains references from the school committee and her new place is secured. As she waits for the carrier to collect her trunk, Bessie arrives.
- Bessie tells Jane what has been happening at Gateshead and says that seven years ago a Mr Eyre, Jane's uncle, had visited the hall looking for her, but had then gone abroad on business.
- The next day, Jane leaves for her new job.

ANALYSIS

A TURNING POINT

The chapter opens with a discussion of the form of the novel, the observation that **'this is not to be a regular autobiography'** (p. 99) in order to explain that eight years pass at Lowood before the next series of events unfold. After the dramatic conclusion of the last chapter, here the early part of Jane's life is neatly tied up. She reflects on her time at Lowood, we are reminded of the characters she lived with at Gateshead, and a new character, Mr Eyre, is introduced. Jane is about to enter a new phase of her life. The chapter captures a moment at which Jane seems to grow psychologically. As she throws off her Lowood training, Jane realises that she has the inner resources to escape and **'surmount'** the **'blue peaks'** (p. 101) that she sees ahead of her, a light **sublime** touch.

STUDY FOCUS: REPETITION A01

The use of repetition – **'I desired liberty; for liberty I gasped; for liberty I uttered a prayer'** (p. 102) – is demonstrative of Jane's strength of feeling, especially given the use of **'liberty'** – a word evocative of the French Revolution (1789). Consider the use of repetition elsewhere in the novel.

CRITICAL VIEWPOINT A04

Although, at the time, liberty was thought to be more applicable to men, women like Mary Wollstonecraft in her *Vindication of the Rights of Woman* (1792) fought for it to be extended to women. It is therefore quite telling that Jane settles in the end for **'A new servitude'** (p. 102).

Bessie effectively asks Jane to show off her 'accomplishments'. It was deemed important at this time for a young lady to have acquired 'accomplishments', which generally consisted of decorative, but essentially impractical skills such as playing the piano and watercolour painting. A very well-educated girl like Jane Eyre would also have studied at least one foreign language, and should be able to entertain in 'polite' society.

JANE'S TALENTS

Jane's demonstration of her musical talent for Bessie prefigures her doing the same later at Thornfield in Chapter XIII. She has all the skills required of a governess, and later a schoolmistress, but her drawings and paintings in particular represent her creativity. Later, it is her name on one of her drawings (see Chapters XXXII–XXXIII) that gives away her identity to St John Rivers, suggesting a strong link between her artistic and her true self.

STUDY FOCUS: A 'KIND FAIRY' **A02**

The heart of the novel lies in Jane's descriptions of what is going on in her own mind. Her feelings, especially 'Conscience' and 'Passion' (Chapter XXVII, p. 343), are often given their own voice. These moments of **personification** help us to understand why Jane acts as she does. In this instance a 'kind fairy' (p. 103) seems to tell her what to do to get a new situation. The use of the word also **foreshadows** Rochester's descriptions of Jane once she has her new job – see Chapter XIV.

KEY QUOTATION: CHAPTER X **A01**

'You are genteel enough; you look like a lady, and it is as much as I ever expected of you: you were no beauty as a child.' (p. 108)

Possible interpretations:

- Bessie's observations about Jane at the age of eighteen relate back to her observations of her at the age of ten. Following Jane's clear distress at having been locked in the red-room, Bessie defended Jane, but conceded to Abbot that 'a beauty like Miss Georgiana would be more moving in the same condition.' (p. 31)

- Bessie remains quite realistic about Jane's appearance, but is sympathetic to her, and also remains her confidant and her honest supporter – it is she who carries news to Jane of goings on in Gateshead.

- Bessie's realistic appraisal and constancy together mean that we as readers can rely on her; she validates Jane's **narrative** and observations.

GLOSSARY

102	**stimulus**	stimulation
107	**watch**	stay awake
108	**plucked**	failed exam(s)

CHAPTER XI

SUMMARY

- The chapter opens with Jane waiting in the George Inn at Millcote to be met by someone from Thornfield Hall.
- She finally arrives at Thornfield late at night. She is met there by Mrs Fairfax, who is very cordial and Jane feels quite comfortable.
- The next day she learns that a Mr Rochester is master of the house and that her pupil, Miss Adèle Varens, is his ward. Mr Rochester seldom visits the house, but he is well liked and respected.
- Jane is shown around the house and while descending from the attic hears an eerie laugh.

ANALYSIS

JANE BECOMES A GOVERNESS

By this point Jane Eyre has become an accomplished young woman, as suggested by Bessie in the previous chapter; however, as a governess she is placed in an awkward social position, below the family but above the servants. In this chapter Jane leaves her childhood and schooling behind her and enters young adulthood, 'inexperienced youth' (p. 111). The opening lines – 'A new chapter in a novel' (p. 111) – make it clear that we are reading a work of fiction, despite the book's original subtitle, 'An Autobiography'. However, because of this clarification we are no longer sure that we know who our **narrator** is; is it still Jane Eyre or is it someone else? Several new characters are introduced – Mrs Fairfax, Adèle Varens, Mr Rochester, Grace Poole – and numerous events are **foreshadowed**.

STUDY FOCUS: THORNFIELD   A02

It is worth paying attention to the description of the house and grounds, as there are many close associations between them and their master, Mr Rochester. Though a great house, Thornfield is not all neatly clipped domesticity. Its name is reflected in the 'array of mighty old thorn trees, strong, knotty, and broad as oaks' (p. 118) in its grounds, and the fact that the garden is visually linked to the fields that surround the estate suggests that Thornfield has its wilder aspects and contrasts with the walled regimented garden at Lowood. Jane sleeps well in her small, 'modern' (p. 116) room, but the rest of the house is eerily empty without its master and seems to harbour secrets. At the end of the chapter the description of the attic, the reference to an eerie laugh and the allusion to Bluebeard add to the **Gothic** tone of the Thornfield section of the text. Do they also foreshadow the fact that Rochester is already married to a mentally ill woman whom he keeps locked away on the third floor?

GLOSSARY

113	**romantic**	wild landscape
121	**'La Ligue … Fontaine'**	one of the animal fables of the French author Jean de la Fontaine
123	**spar**	crystal
123	**Tyrian-dyed**	coloured a reddish purple
123	**Parian**	white marble
126	**syllabic**	speech-like

CONTEXT   A03

'Bluebeard' is a fairy story in which a young wife is allowed to enter any room she wants in her husband's castle except one. When he leaves the castle on business one day she takes the keys and investigates. In the room she finds the bodies of his previous wives. This story has formed a focus for many feminist writers, especially Angela Carter. You find a re-telling of the Bluebeard story in Carter's 'The Bloody Chamber', published in her 1979 collection of the same name.

CHAPTER XII

SUMMARY

- Jane settles in.
- When she is bored she goes for walks or climbs to the attic and longs for excitement and thinks of other people's 'rebellions' (p. 129).
- One day she walks to Hay to deliver a letter. It is very cold and as she rests she sees a horse and rider slip on some ice. She helps the man remount his horse and continues on her errand.
- When she returns to the hall she discovers that the man she helped was her employer, Mr Rochester.

ANALYSIS

THE ATTIC

Jane's visits to the attic help form an imaginative link between Jane Eyre and Mrs Rochester, as in the red-room. Jane sees a ghost in the red-room and hears strange, ghostly sounds in the attic at Thornfield. The red-room and the attic are meant to be disused, uninhabited and empty, and take on uncanny, eerie qualities. Brontë perhaps suggests that if Jane fell victim to her passions, or even if she became mistress of the house, she might become as undisciplined and alienated from society as her rival in the attic.

JANE MEETS MR ROCHESTER

The scene in which Jane and Rochester meet for the first time is dramatic and its outcome, when he finds that 'necessity compels me to make you useful' (p. 136), **foreshadows** his ultimate physical dependence on her. As we can see from her assumption that Rochester's dog is the 'Gytrash' (p. 132), Jane's imagination is full of fiends, and the fact that she is sensitive to omens becomes particularly important in Chapter XXXV.

STUDY FOCUS: FIRE AND ICE **A02**

It is significant that Jane and Rochester meet over ice, and that later she finds the fires lit at Thornfield where the grates had stood empty. Indeed, until Rochester arrives, to return to Thornfield is 'to return to stagnation' (p. 137). Jane does not want the trappings of conventional femininity; as she says herself, she is 'becoming incapable of appreciating' the 'very privileges of security and ease' (p. 137) her job at Thornfield have given her. Under Rochester's power she will begin to melt and unlearn much of her Lowood reserve. Look elsewhere in the novel for the use of fire and ice.

GLOSSARY

132   **'Gytrash'** huge black, shaggy dog from **folklore** that appears in churchyards and lonely lanes at dusk. If it looks you in the eye, you are warned of the death of a relative or friend

136   **'Like heath … away'** Thomas Moore, 'Fallen is the throne…' II.19–20

137   **'too easy chair'** Alexander Pope, *Dunciad*, IV.343

CHAPTER XIII

SUMMARY

- Thornfield is enlivened by visitors who come to do business with Mr Rochester.
- At the end of the day Jane and Adèle are invited to take tea with the master who interrogates Jane about her history, asks her to play the piano and requires her to show him her sketches.

ANALYSIS

MR ROCHESTER: A BYRONIC HERO

Mr Rochester is a **Romantic**, almost Byronic, figure who, in this chapter, is shown to be forceful and independent; in this respect he is in part Jane's alter ego. A Byronic hero is so called after the poet Byron, and refers to a charismatic yet brooding and cynical character. Having travelled, seeking exotic adventure, such a character often harbours a secret, about which he has no real shame. A Byronic hero is proud, sets himself apart from society's norms and values, but, despite being rebellious and quite menacing, remains fascinating to others. This, as we will see, exactly describes Rochester.

STUDY FOCUS: JANE'S UNCONVENTIONAL BEHAVIOUR **A02**

Jane and Rochester's convincing and witty banter brings both characters alive. She may have feminine accomplishments, but she is as unconventional and strong-minded as he is and can always match him blow for blow in any conversation. Rochester often refers to Jane as a fairy, a sprite and an imp: 'When you came on me in Hay Lane last night, I thought unaccountably of fairy tales' (p. 143) but he eventually learns that he must respect her as an individual. Consider the degree to which this was a marked departure from the literary (and social) conventions of the day.

Jane's paintings reflect the Romantic preoccupation with extreme, wild landscapes and exotica and echo the landscapes of the book she was reading in the opening chapter. They are also indicative of her true nature.

CONTEXT **A03**

Heathcliff in Emily Brontë's *Wuthering Heights* (1847) is another classic example of a Byronic hero. *Wuthering Heights* was published just a month after *Jane Eyre*. The two novels were often assumed to be by the same author, and Charlotte Brontë worked hard to defend the reputation of her work from its association with her sister's. *Wuthering Heights* was generally seen as much more risqué.

GLOSSARY

139	**prenomens**	first and second names
142	**piquant**	stimulating
144	**'men in green'**	fairies always wear the colour green
145	**'head and front of his offending'**	Shakespeare, *Othello*, I.3.80
146	**'Approach the table'**	bring the table closer
146	**copies**	originals
148	**'the likeness ... none'**	Milton, *Paradise Lost*, II.666–73
148	**Latmos**	mountain in Turkey (Besh Parmark), where, in classical legend, the goddess of the moon, Silene, fell in love with Endymion

CHAPTER XIV

SUMMARY

- After a few days Jane and Adèle are again called in to spend the evening with Rochester, who gives Adèle a box of toys and a dress.
- Jane and Rochester engage in another sparring conversation, this time about his appearance, their relative social positions and morality.

ANALYSIS

MR ROCHESTER AND JANE SPAR WITH EACH OTHER

The chapter begins in a characteristically **journalistic** style. These descriptive passages draw us into the action, and are often highly suggestive. However, though the language used is simple and direct – and while the dialogue is generally quite convincing and naturalistic – much of the tenor of the conversation that takes place here is evocative of fairy stories like 'The Beauty and the Beast'.

STUDY FOCUS: SPEECH AND LANGUAGE **A02**

Jane and Rochester's conversations allow us to learn a great deal about his character, attitudes and state of mind.

The way in which the different characters speak usually reflects their education and station, and with respect to Adèle it is also indicative of her nationality and training. The extensive use of French in the novel adds authenticity to Adèle's exchanges with Jane. Does it also make Jane's own accomplishments more tangible to the reader?

NO PHILANTHROPIST

Again, we have a phrenological moment (see **Part Two: Chapter VIII**) when Rochester holds up the hair from his forehead in order for Jane to inspect his 'intellectual organs', though as he notes there is 'an abrupt deficiency where the suave sign of benevolence should have risen' (p. 154). It is on this basis that Jane implies he is no 'philanthropist' (p. 154), which suggests that his kindness towards her – in letting her sit with him after dinner, despite the difference in their stations – is not done out of charity. His statement that he bears 'a conscience' (p. 155) is perhaps borne out by his attempt to save Bertha when the house burns down.

GLOSSARY

153	**interlocutrice**	female companion in conversation
154	*nonnette*	little nun
139	**'bad eminence'**	Milton, *Paradise Lost*, II.6

CHAPTER XV

SUMMARY

- As they walk in the hall's grounds, Rochester tells Jane about his relationship with Adèle's mother and how he came to look after Adèle after her mother abandoned her.
- Jane lies awake reflecting on their discussion.
- Jane no longer thinks that Rochester is ugly. Now he brightens up her life.
- When she goes to investigate a strange noise she discovers that Rochester's bed has been set alight.
- Jane puts the fire out. Rochester goes to find the arsonist and on his return Grace Poole's name is mentioned.
- Rochester prefers to compliment Jane on her actions rather than talk about the fire.
- Before they part he confesses that he feels a natural sympathy for Jane.

ANALYSIS

JANE SAVES MR ROCHESTER

This chapter forms the end of the first volume (in the first edition of the book – see **Part One:** *Jane Eyre* **in context**) and marks a clear alteration in Rochester and Jane's relationship. The fire **foreshadows** the destruction of Thornfield as outlined in Chapter XXXVI and, with Jane's speculation about Rochester, generates a sense of suspense. Again, Rochester is shown to need Jane who seems to know him better than he knows himself. He seems unable to express himself, and his true feelings are revealed as he begins to lose fluency. We know Jane's hopes and fears because we are given a privileged insight into her innermost thoughts; we know his through conversation and what he does not say.

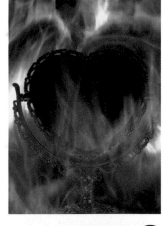

STUDY FOCUS: FIRE `A02`

The fire **symbolises** raging passion, either Bertha's or Rochester's, doused by Jane's Christian temperance – she 'baptise[s] the couch' – though Rochester accuses her of being a 'witch, sorceress' (p. 174). This last **image** draws on *Medea* – possibly a more apt description of Bertha Mason than Jane Eyre. Again, Bertha and Jane are linked imaginatively; though one sets and the other douses the fire, Rochester can hardly tell the difference. Look elsewhere in the novel for the use of fire.

GLOSSARY

165	**Apollo Belvidere**	famous statue of Apollo in the Vatican
	hotel	town house
165	**dentelles**	lace
165	**spoony**	demonstratively fond lover
167	**'Job's leviathan ... habergeon'**	Job 41:26
168	**'heart's core'**	Shakespeare, *Hamlet*, III.2.73
169	**extinguisher**	of candle
169	**chicken in the pip**	diseased chicken
177	**Beulah**	an idyllic place, see Isaiah 62:4 and Bunyan, *The Pilgrim's Progress*

CONTEXT `A03`

The Medea legend is complex, with many endings, but crucially Medea is a sorceress whose husband Jason eventually loses interest in her and marries someone else, Creusa/Glauce, the daughter of the King of Corinth. Medea takes revenge by killing Creusa with a poisoned coronet. In his play (*Medea*, 431 BCE) Euripides rewrote the tale, adding that after taking revenge Medea also stabbed her two children by Jason.

CHAPTER XVI

SUMMARY

- The next morning Jane sees Grace Poole, the suspected arsonist, helping to restore Rochester's room.
- When Jane confronts her she warns Jane to keep her door locked at night. Jane is puzzled by this and hopes to ask Rochester about it.
- Jane finds out that Rochester has gone away to visit some friends. Mrs Fairfax describes some of the people he will meet, including Blanche Ingram, and Jane realises that she has been foolish in thinking she could be one of his favourites.
- Jane paints a self-portrait called 'Portrait of a Governess, disconnected, poor, and plain' (p. 187).

ANALYSIS

JANE TRIES TO COME TO HER SENSES

The suspense generated in the previous chapter is maintained and our curiosity is aroused by Jane's strange conversation with Grace. People are not quite what they seem. Events in Chapter XXV are **foreshadowed** when Grace warns Jane to lock her door. It becomes clear that Jane is falling in love with Rochester, and her method of handling him once they are engaged is suggested here in her self-assured pleasure at '**vexing and soothing him**' (p. 183). But in the meantime Jane is very hard on herself, calling herself a '**dupe**', and '**Blind puppy**' (p. 186). In this way, Jane quells her feelings, as she learned to do at Lowood. Several new characters are introduced and help highlight Jane's ambiguous social position.

STUDY FOCUS: APPEARANCES   A04

It is worth noting how Jane expresses her feelings through art, and how she holds the described beauty of Blanche Ingram up against her own plain form. As suggested by the title she gives to her portrait, she cannot realistically hope to marry Rochester because of the difference in class, but, initially at least, Blanche is also described as the pinnacle of beauty and Jane is well aware that she cannot compete on these terms – see the earlier discussion between Bessie and Abbot about Jane's looks and their impact (Chapter III). In this case, consider the ways in which femininity is linked to appearance.

'PORTRAIT OF A GOVERNESS'

Jane Eyre picks up on the **image** of and issues surrounding the governess. This painful and isolating position was widely commented on at the time and the governess's plight was well known. But, it would have been quite scandalous for a governess to spend time with her employer in the way that Jane does. In this sense, she is in a fairy story where the social norms are suspended – perhaps playing the part of Cinderella.

GLOSSARY

178	**momentarily**	moment by moment
186	**unvarnished tale**	Shakespeare, *Othello*, I.3.90

CHAPTER XVII

SUMMARY

- After a fortnight Rochester's friends come to stay at Thornfield. The house is prepared and extra servants are brought in.
- During the preparations, Jane overhears part of a conversation about Grace Poole, but cannot make much sense of it as she is deliberately excluded from the mystery.
- The visitors soon arrive; the house is full of guests, servants, hustle and bustle.
- The next day, Jane and Adèle are invited to join the party after dinner. As the ladies chatter and all engage in the evening's amusement, Jane watches and overhears a nasty conversation about governesses.
- When Jane slips away Rochester comes after her and insists that she join the party in the drawing room every evening.

ANALYSIS

MISS INGRAM AND FRIENDS VISIT THORNFIELD

The whole of this chapter repays close analysis. For example, what does Rochester want to say when he hesitates: 'Good-night, my –' (p. 210)? Jane's hatred of company was foreshadowed in Chapter IV, but in this instance we are provided with a slice of upper-class life, as observed by someone who sees herself as a social outcast. Jane hides behind the curtain as she did in Chapter I, a position that reflects her marginalised status in both great houses, but in this case allows her, as **narrator**, privileged access to others' conversations.

STUDY FOCUS: GOVERNESSES — A04

The fact that Jane is a governess herself gives an edge to the conversation: 'You should hear mama on the chapter of governesses; Mary and I have had … a dozen at least in our day; half of them detestable and the rest ridiculous, and all incubi' (p. 205). This exchange plays on several issues surrounding the governess in the 1840s: their cost, their morality and their ability to maintain standards, and their susceptibility. The governess, it was supposed, was liable to both mental illness and to seduction, and was therefore often despised by her social superiors. Do you think that this was something of which, as a governess, Charlotte Brontë was well aware?

REFLECTING ON THE PAST

The frequent use of the present tense gives Jane's descriptions immediacy and draws us into the scene. However, because Jane's narrative is written some years after the event she can also reflect more maturely and quite humorously on her adolescent attempts to 'master' herself and dismiss her highly inappropriate feelings. This could also be said to add to the part that **irony** plays in the novel.

CONTEXT — A04

As Charlotte Brontë herself observed: 'None but those who had been in the position of a governess could ever realise that dark side of "respectable" human nature; under no great temptation to crime, but daily giving way to selfishness and ill-temper, till its conduct toward those dependent on it sometimes amounts to a tyranny of which one would rather be the victim than the inflicter.' (Elizabeth Gaskell, *The Life of Charlotte Brontë* (1857), Chapter 9).

KEY QUOTATION: CHAPTER XVII   A01

Mrs Fairfax: 'I'll tell you how to manage so as to avoid the embarrassment of making a formal entrance, which is the most disagreeable part of the business.' (p. 197)

Possible interpretations:

- Via Mrs Fairfax, Rochester has insisted that Jane join the party, even though they are 'all strangers' and even though Mrs Fairfax has explained that Jane was 'unused to company' (p. 197). Mrs Fairfax is trying to help Jane in this awkward social situation.

- Jane's need of advice about how to cope with company and her withdrawn behaviour in social situations stand out in the novel and make her quite idiosyncratic. Her difficulties in social settings – her puzzlement and awkwardness in the face of social convention – were interpreted by some on publication as rudeness, but her modest behaviour might also have been seen as appropriate to her sex.

- Jane's social unease, isolation, dislocation and silence have been interpreted as being grounded in her social class.

STUDY FOCUS: CRITIQUING JANE   A04

Feminist critics have seen Jane's dislocation as representing women's position in society as a whole: disempowered, disconnected and marginalised. Post-colonial readings associate her alienation with the wider dynamics of imperial power in the novel. Critics within disability studies have observed that Jane's characterisation and influence on others is evocative of the experiences of someone on the autistic spectrum. Autistic spectrum disorders, such as autism and Asperger syndrome, are very variable and wide ranging in the ways they present, but commonly include difficulties with social interaction, social communication and social imagination. Jane's inherent loneliness has also been seen as originating in the **Gothic** – she is strange and by drawing the reader in, her character enables them to reflect on social norms by making them seem unfamiliar.

CONTEXT   A04

'Succubus' (a female demon that descends upon a man as he sleeps from the Latin for 'to lie under) might be more apt than 'incubus' (a male demon) given recent events. The error goes to show Blanche Ingram's ignorance of the real situation and may also work as a possible comment on her flawed education.

GLOSSARY

194	**'Some natural tears she shed'** Milton, *Paradise Lost*, XII, 645
199	*'minois chiffoné'* with charming irregularity
205	**incubi** from the Latin for nightmare, something that weights heavily on the mind, but also a male demon that descends upon women as they sleep
206	**'in the pip'** bad tempered
207	**quiz** tease
207	**Rizzio ... Mary** David Rizzio, Italian singer, Mary Queen of Scots's secretary and lover
207	**black Bothwell ... James Hepburn** Earl of Bothwell who murdered Mary Queen of Scots's first husband in order to marry her
208	**Corsairs** Byron, *The Corsairs* (1814). Some confusion exists as to the date at which the novel is set

CHAPTER XVIII

SUMMARY

- The party stays on and engages in a variety of pastimes, including a game of charades.
- Jane is convinced that Rochester will marry Miss Ingram for her 'rank and connections' (p. 216).
- While Rochester is absent a stranger, Mr Mason, calls to see him.
- While Mason waits for Rochester's return an old gypsy woman appears and insists on telling 'the gentry their fortunes' (p. 223). Eventually, all of the ladies go to her and have their fortunes told.

ANALYSIS

A GAME OF CHARADES, A STRANGER AND A GYPSY

The stress of the chapter lies on appearances and disguises. The stage-like entrances and exits of the previous chapter are played on in the game of charades, and in the dramatic arrival of the stranger and old gypsy woman. Jane's reflections on social convention and the necessity of marrying for love are important when she comes to consider St John Rivers's proposal in Chapter XXXIV. More significantly, a charade of a marriage – Rochester seems to specialise in mock marriages – and the arrival of a stranger are distinctly ominous.

STUDY FOCUS: JANE'S OPINION OF MISS INGRAM **A02**

Jane's opinion of Miss Ingram is quite condescending; though she acknowledges that the latter is her social superior. She asserts that she is not jealous – despite the best efforts of Rochester who seems determined to flirt with Miss Ingram quite outrageously – because she does not think Rochester loves the heiress and the heiress is all show. It is worth considering whether Jane is quite the reliable **narrator** in this instance, and noting that Jane can see Rochester – the man she loves – as capable of financial or political self-interest in this case, but not amorous self-interest later on.

GRADE BOOSTER **A02**

Consider the parallels that are drawn between the women in the novel. Rochester married Bertha Mason for money and Jane believes that he would marry Blanche Ingram for her position. The description of Miss Ingram as 'a real strapper … big, brown and buxom' (p. 253) suggests that she looks just like Bertha, and in many respects Miss Ingram also behaves like Bertha before Rochester married her.

GLOSSARY

211–12 **sacques … modes … lappets** all eighteenth-century items of women's dress

212 **pantomime** mime or silent play acting

213 **Paynim** pagan

213 **bowstring** used by assassins

222 **old Mother Bunches** Mother Bunch was a byword for jests and old wives' tales

225 **the old gentleman** the devil

225 **sibyl** female prophet

225 **'I am sure … not right'** Goldsmith, *Vicar of Wakefield*

CHAPTER XIX

SUMMARY

- Jane meets the gypsy who seems bent on asking her questions rather than telling her fortune, which makes Jane suspicious.
- The gypsy reads Jane's face then asks her to go. Jane hesitates and realises that the gypsy is actually Mr Rochester.
- When he hears that Mr Mason has arrived in his absence he is stunned, but when everyone retires all seems well.

CONTEXT **A04**

The gypsy fortune-teller episode plays on the dominant stereotype of the gypsy, while Roma or gypsies themselves remained a marginalised group. Though a treatise calling for the better treatment of gypsies was written by a Quaker, John Hoyland, in 1816, gypsies camping on the roadside were fined when the Turnpike Act of 1822 came into force.

ANALYSIS

JANE AND THE GYPSY

Jane and the gypsy's conversation begins in a way that mirrors Jane's conversation with Mr Brocklehurst in Chapter IV and is again reminiscent of 'Little Red Riding Hood': 'You've a quick ear.' 'I have; and a quick eye, and a quick brain' (p. 227). Contrast the gypsy's assessment of Jane as 'cold', 'sick' and 'silly' (p. 228) with Jane's own insistence that she is 'disconnected, poor, and plain' (Chapter XVI, p. 187). Notice how, as the conversation between them becomes more intimate, Jane moves closer to the fortune-teller (Rochester) who stirs the fire to light her up, though she later complains 'the fire scorches me' (p. 232). This further suggests that Rochester kindles passion in Jane. His reading of her nature, of the way 'passions may rage furiously … but judgment shall still have the last word in every argument' (p. 233) tells us that he is a close observer and captures the essence of her character. Later, when she leaves Thornfield it is indeed because she listens to 'that still small voice which interprets the dictates of conscience' (p. 233). It is this sense of propriety that he tries to undermine, and which causes her to say of the penetrative interview: 'it was not right' (p. 234). Jane is angry at Rochester for the loss of control this entails, at the way her story has been stolen from her by the gypsy. But, this is the most intimate scene between them so far.

STUDY FOCUS: CONNECTIONS   **A02**

The unveiling of Mr Rochester is dramatically and **symbolically** significant, further developing the theme of charade. With the arrival of Mr Mason, we move closer to the mystery at the heart of Thornfield, and Rochester's actual unveiling. Rochester's declaration that he has 'got a blow' (p. 235) and his leaning on Jane echoes the scene when she helped him after the fall from his horse and **foreshadows** his later dependence on her. Think about the other ways in which minor characters like Mason allow connections to be drawn between the different sections of the novel.

GLOSSARY

228	**'nichered'**	laughed, like a horse
232	**blackaviced**	dark-skinned
233	**'The passions may rage … things'**	Psalms, 2:1
233	**'Strong wind … voice'**	I Kings 19:11–12
233	**'the play is played out'**	untraced quotation
233	**Did I dream still?**	Keats, 'Ode to a Nightingale', ll.79–80
234	**eld**	old
234	**'Off, ye lendings!'**	Shakespeare, *King Lear*, III.4.111

CHAPTER XX

SUMMARY

- Jane hears a cry, a struggle and a call for help.

- Once he has pacified his guests, Rochester asks Jane to follow him into the attic and leaves her to nurse Mr Mason whose arm and shoulder are soaked in blood.

- She and Mr Mason are sworn to silence while Rochester fetches a surgeon and, while she waits, Jane speculates about what has happened.

- As dawn comes Rochester returns and the doctor quickly dresses Mason's wounds.

- Mason is spirited away and Jane is left puzzling over events but Rochester begins one of his moral conversations. Finally he starts talking about marrying Miss Ingram.

ANALYSIS

THE MYSTERY DEEPENS

Because Jane is unable to follow any of the conversations that take place around her or what Rochester says to her, neither can we. Thornfield Hall, which is always symbolically important, becomes more mysterious, more **Gothic**. Notice how Thornfield and its owner, who still seems to be playing charades, are linked (see **The chestnut tree** in **Part Four: Imagery and symbolism**). Jane is morally direct and sure-footed; she will only 'obey' (p. 250) Rochester if it is right to do so and this becomes important at the end of the volume (see **Part One: *Jane Eyre* in context**). The full moon is clearly associated with the lunatic antics of Mrs Rochester, who behaves like a vampire (see **Part Two: Chapter XXV**).

A SPRING MORNING

The horrors of the attic are contrasted with the peace of the garden in the early morning. The fresh 'old-fashioned flowers' (p. 249) generate scent that evokes a sense of freedom and wild nature. Despite the April showers, the scene in the garden – especially the phrase 'You have passed a strange night, Jane' (p. 249) – evokes Shakespeare's *A Midsummer Night's Dream*, a **motif** that is more fully explored in Chapter XXIII. Where Jane seeks the advice of a 'good spirit', she wishes for Ariel to speak to her in the 'breath' of the west wind (p. 252). Jane will later hear the moon advise her to 'flee temptation' in Chapter XXVII (p. 367). Later still, she will hear Rochester's voice calling her back and Rochester will hear her reply.

GLOSSARY

238	**curtain**	bed curtain
242	**mystic**	mysterious, strange
244	**outraged**	attacked
249	**glamour**	enchantment
252	**'your sun at noon … eclipse'**	Milton, *Samson Agonistes*, ll.80–1
252	**Ariel**	in literature, Ariel is commonly referred to as a spirit, e.g. in Milton's *Paradise Lost* (1667) Ariel is a rebellious angel, in Shakespeare's *Tempest* Ariel is 'an ayrie spirit'
253	**Carthage**	in St Augustine's *Confessions*, a city of debauchery

CHAPTER XXI

SUMMARY

- Jane is unsettled by a recurring dream about an infant and sees it as a bad omen.
- She is summoned to Gateshead by her aunt who is very ill. Her cousin John has died in mysterious circumstances. Rochester is reluctant to let her go, but she finally gets a leave of absence.
- While talking to Rochester she asks him to find her another situation before he marries.
- Her arrival at Gateshead brings back memories; she is welcomed by Bessie though Miss Eliza and Miss Georgiana are less agreeable.
- Jane insists on seeing her aunt who is very confused. Some days later her aunt gives her a three-year-old letter from John Eyre, her uncle, who wanted to adopt her.
- Jane refers to Mrs Reed as 'aunt' (p. 266), but despite Jane's attempts at kindness there can be no reconciliation.
- Mrs Reed dies.

ANALYSIS

JANE DREAMS

The chapter begins in reflective mood and moves on into the structure of 'The Beauty and the Beast'. We are filled in on the recent history of the Reeds, which provides a link back to the beginning of the book and allows Jane to complete the business of her childhood. Her aunt's use of the third person when talking to Jane – 'I have had more trouble with that child than anyone would believe' (p. 267) – allows us to gain some understanding of Mrs Reed's point of view. Jane tries to behave as Helen Burns would have done, but learns that she must be true to herself and that people do not change in the way her religious schooling suggests that they should.

STUDY FOCUS: CATHOLICISM   A02

Jane's cousins represent two opposing kinds of conventional femininity: one that has the sole aim of marrying to advantage (Georgiana), the other that is self-sacrificing and inclined to retreat from the world onto the moral high ground (Eliza). Jane herself detests all things that are aligned with popish Catholicism, as opposed to what was perceived as good English Protestantism. Jane is a traditionalist. Though this can be read in part as being about Charlotte Brontë's faith, do these anti-Catholic overtones also fit in with the Gothic elements of the novel as a whole – eighteenth-century Gothic novels often being anti-Catholic?

SIGNS

The reference at the beginning of the chapter to 'Presentiments', 'sympathies' and 'signs' (p. 254) becomes particularly pertinent in Chapter XXXV, but Jane's sensitivity to all kinds of omens is often used to **foreshadow** events and helps drive the plot, add **irony** and create suspense. Uncanny **imagery** and **symbolism** help pull the different parts of the novel together into an organic whole. Jane's uncle becomes important in Chapter XXVI and Chapter XXXIII.

CONTEXT   A03

Jane has learned how to interpret dreams from Bessie, the servant, and this is a typical **Gothic motif** – in Gothic novels it is servants, especially old nursemaids, who generally teach their charges about **folklore** and the supernatural.

GRADE BOOSTER   A02

Consider the use of dreams in this novel as a way of foreshadowing events, creating irony and suspense, and moving the plot along. This will demonstrate that you have a good understanding of form.

CHAPTER XXII

SUMMARY

- A month later Jane leaves Gateshead.
- Georgiana eventually marries. Eliza sets off for France to become a nun.
- When she returns to Thornfield, Jane is surprised by her feelings for Rochester and discloses that she would rather not leave him again.
- There is a rumour that Rochester is about to marry, but few preparations are being made.

ANALYSIS

ELIZA REED

Eliza Reed has been shown to be quite heartless; she is focused entirely on the small details of life and works diligently to complete all the little jobs that she sets out to do. She is well aware of what constitutes proper and improper behaviour but has no interest in the metaphysical, the spiritual or even the feeling aspects of human life. She is uncharitable and uncaring. Her freely made decision to go to a convent is therefore a critique of the Catholic religion, especially as she is so successful in her vocation.

STUDY FOCUS: THORNFIELD {A02}

The use of the present tense, as Jane approaches Thornfield Hall, gives the whole scene immediacy. Thornfield reappears under its pleasantest aspect and at the beginning of summer: an appropriate time and setting for courtship. The suggestion may be that Thornfield and its master together make up 'home'.

CHECK THE FILM {A04}

There have been at least eighteen film versions of the novel. *Jane Eyre* (2011) directed by Cary Fukunaga, screenplay by Moira Buffini, is one of the latest. This particular version of *Jane Eyre* is incredibly detailed in its depiction of the interior and exterior settings. The film unusually also allows time for Jane to establish her relationship with the Rivers family, and the casting reflects the ages of the characters in the novel.

CHAPTER XXIII

SUMMARY

- Jane meets Rochester as she walks in the grounds on Midsummer-eve, and he engages her in conversation.
- He says that she must leave Thornfield as he will soon marry. She begins to cry.
- They sit under the old chestnut tree and he suddenly confesses that he has no intention of marrying Miss Ingram. He actually wants to marry Jane.
- Jane doubts and quizzes him, but finally accepts him.
- During the night a great storm splits the old chestnut tree in two.

ANALYSIS

ROCHESTER PROPOSES

The chapter opens with two references to Midsummer in quick succession. Midsummer itself is a pivotal point in the year, but this also evokes Shakespeare's *A Midsummer Night's Dream*: a story of sprites and star-crossed lovers. The chapter then provides us with the first climax of the novel. The language is heightened and passionate – quite **journalistic** where Jane cannot express her emotion – and the tone is one of foreboding. Rochester's observation that a moth reminds him of a 'West Indian insect' (p. 288) gestures towards the later revelation that Rochester is married to a Creole (see **Glossary** in **Part Two: Chapter XXVI**). The storm suggests that God will not pardon Rochester or sanction his actions – he is still in effect living a lie, even though the charade of an engagement with Miss Ingram is over. But, there is humour here too in Rochester's suggestion that Jane educate 'the five daughters of Mrs Dionysius O'Gall of Bitternutt Lodge' (p. 290). The fact that he is teasing her is made clear in the names 'O'Gall' and 'Bitternutt', but this is quite subtle and she remains ignorant of his real intent.

STUDY FOCUS: THE OLD CHESTNUT TREE A02

Thornfield and its grounds are closely associated with their master – we can see this in the way that the scent of Rochester's cigar mingles with that of the flowers. Is the fact that the old tree is split in two ominous, given that the tree is **symbolic** of Jane and Rochester's relationship?

GLOSSARY

186	**'Day its fervid … wasted'**	Thomas Campbell, 'The Turkish Lady', l.5
289	**lady-clock** (**dialect**)	lady-bird; (children's rhyme) 'Lady-bird, lady-bird fly away home,/Your house is on fire,/Your children all flown'
290	**Dionysius**	was common in the Catholic church as a name of Saints, monks and members of the clergy
292	**'morsel of bread … living water'**	(biblical) refers to Communion

EXTENDED COMMENTARY

CHAPTER XXIII, PP. 291–3

From '"Come! we'll talk over"' to '"all my possessions."'

As Jane gradually moves, Eve-like, from innocence to understanding we are provided with a lyrical example of the naturalistic dialogue that regularly takes place between the two lovers. Their conversations bring the characters alive and through them Charlotte Brontë makes a complete break with the novels of her time. Where other authors avoided this kind of complex exchange, by glossing over the characters' speeches or using paraphrase, and some produced only a stilted and clumsy impression of speech, Charlotte Brontë manages to move rapidly and confidently between confusion, explanation and exclamation in such a way as to allow us to understand Jane's turmoil and Rochester's inner conflict.

Jane is quite powerless, given her social position, but speaks as an individual who demands to be treated with respect and fights to maintain her identity – 'I am no bird; … I am a free human being with an independent will' (p. 293) – and so talks on behalf of her sex. She does not want to be exiled, but fights for her self-respect by demanding that she be permitted to leave rather than watch Rochester enter a conventional marriage based on property. In the process she recites her history to date 'I have not been trampled on. I have not been petrified. I have not been buried with inferior minds' (p. 292). She is trying to reconcile passion with duty, 'and it is like looking on the necessity of death' (p. 292).

Rochester, half talking to Jane, half thinking out loud – 'if I can't do better, how is it to be helped?' (p. 291) – tests her love and is working up to asking her for her hand. The reason for his hesitation becomes clear on their wedding day, and is unwittingly **foreshadowed** by Jane – 'you are a married man … and wed to one inferior to you' (p. 293) – while she still thinks he intends to marry Miss Ingram. **Ironically**, Miss Ingram does in fact look like and behave as his wife did before her mental breakdown.

CHECK THE BOOK **A03**

For a detailed discussion of the relationship between the woman writer and the idea of her 'mad' double – in fictional form – see S. M. Gilbert and S. Gubar *The Madwoman in the Attic: The Woman Writer and the Nineteenth-Century Literary Imagination* (1979).

In loving Jane, Rochester hopes to find Bertha's direct opposite – 'the antipodes of the Creole' (Chapter XXVII, p. 358) (see **Glossary** in **Part Two: Chapter XXVI**). Though Jane has begun to mature and combine passion with self-control, Rochester has yet to learn from his experiences or face the consequences of his actions. As he pours out his love against the nightingale's song, he still needs to realise that Jane will only love him in return if he treats her with respect. Though his love is quite genuine, his proposal is essentially built on a secret and is therefore enslaving, dishonourable and shallow: the Midsummer's fairy tale is about to be exposed as a sham.

At this point Jane and Rochester are doomed, as is suggested in the storm that breaks out over their heads. The chestnut tree under which Jane and Rochester sit is a **symbol** of life, but quickly becomes an omen of ill-fortune and they are chased out of the paradisiacal garden as Rochester asks God to sanction their marriage. The Thornfield section of the novel is often simultaneously personal and symbolic in this way. Rochester gives Thornfield Hall life and a sense of purpose when he is there, but it is also symbolically identified with him. When Jane first tours the building there are vague foreshadowings of what she will find out about it and its master. By the end of the novel, when he has finally learnt his lesson, Rochester likens his own maimed body to the shriven tree's black form.

CHECK THE FILM A03

Think about the extent to which Jane finds Thornfield a happy home, despite the disturbing sounds she hears. In his 1996 film, Franco Zeffirelli makes Jane's room light and pleasant, while the regions of the house controlled by Rochester are darker and more sinister.

REVISION FOCUS: TASK 2 A02

How far do you agree with the following statements?

- Landscape, place and nature carry character in *Jane Eyre*.
- In *Jane Eyre*, disability is a real as well as a **metaphorical** condition.

Write opening paragraphs for essays based on these discussion points. Set out your arguments clearly and ensure that your paragraphs link to each other in a logical way.

CHAPTER XXIV

SUMMARY

- The next day Rochester says that they will be married in a month.
- He wants to shower Jane with gifts and take her on a tour of Europe. Jane is wary and does not want to be flattered or dressed in jewels.
- Mrs Fairfax is not entirely easy about what has happened and is worried that something will go wrong.
- Jane, Adèle and Rochester go to Millcote where Jane and Rochester disagree over the choice of dresses and trinkets.
- Jane determines to write to her uncle in order to secure her independence and she insists that she continue as governess for the month of their engagement.
- Jane consistently keeps Rochester at arm's length during the rest of their courtship.

ANALYSIS

ARRANGEMENTS ARE MADE FOR THE WEDDING

The fact that there is trouble ahead is clearly **foreshadowed**, which adds suspense to what is otherwise a straightforward romance. The fact that the **narrator** can drop hints that Rochester is still hiding something – 'as if well pleased at seeing a danger averted' (p. 303) – while Jane ignores them can make the reader feel a little uncomfortable until we remember that the narrative is being told by an older and wiser Jane some time after the event.

> **CONTEXT** **A04**
>
> Dress was seen as being indicative of a woman's morality in the nineteenth century; prostitutes were often said to wear 'finery', especially velvets, feathers and costume jewellery.

STUDY FOCUS: THE ROLE OF MUSIC **A04**

Songs and ballads are inserted into the text in their entirety throughout the novel and bear close examination for their themes and their reception. For example, after being imprisoned in the red-room Jane finds Bessie's gypsy song saddening though she had once enjoyed it at as an adventurous tale. How important are songs and music in the novel?

GLOSSARY

301	**Hercules**	in classical legend Hercules is enslaved by his love for Omphale
301	**Samson**	Samson reveals the secret of his strength to Delilah, his mistress
302	**Ahasuerus**	Persian king who marries a poor Jewish girl, Esther
309	**Danae**	in classical legend, Danae is seduced by Zeus who appears as a shower of gold
310	**three-tailed bashaw**	Turkish ruler
313–4	**The truest love … loved am I**	the song is Charlotte Brontë's

CHAPTER XXV

SUMMARY

- While Jane waits for Rochester's return from business she thinks about an event that happened the previous night.
- Eventually, Rochester arrives and, at midnight, she tells him that an apparition came to her room, and tore the veil he had given her.
- Rochester assures her that she merely saw Grace Poole, and sends her to sleep with Adèle in the nursery.

ANALYSIS

JANE'S PRESCIENCE

This is a **Gothic** chapter, full of foreboding. Jane's prescience (ability to see the future) in her dreams shows her the **motif** of the little child and Thornfield reduced to a shell. Her thoughts on contemplating the ruin of the chestnut tree **foreshadow** her feelings when reunited with Rochester at the end of the novel: 'I think, scathed as you look, … there must be a little sense of life in you yet, rising out of that adhesion at the faithful, honest roots' (p. 319). It is only after Rochester has been 'scorched' (p. 319) that Jane can come to him; for the moment he remains 'ardent and flushed' (p. 322) with desire, in danger of burning out of control.

There is **irony** in Jane's refusal to use the luggage labels because 'Mrs Rochester' does not yet exist, especially when the real Mrs Rochester tears Jane's own veil – although this allows Jane to wear the plain veil she preferred to the excessive one Mr Rochester sent for from London. There are also references to earlier events in the novel, particularly in the red-room and Bertha's attack on her brother, Mr Mason.

STUDY FOCUS: BERTHA ROCHESTER **A03**

This is the first clear sight we have of Bertha Rochester, who until this point has made her presence felt largely by disembodied wails, unseen fire-setting and disavowed violence. She is described as 'discoloured' and 'savage', 'purple' with lips 'swelled and dark' and 'bloodshot eyes' (p. 327). Jane's association of Bertha with a vampire, based  on this appearance, was a commonplace in the nineteenth century – descriptions of vampires closely resembled stereotypes of Jews, cannibals and lunatics. It is a description of the unfamiliar and deviant other that was typical of the time.

GLOSSARY

317	**D.V.** *Deo Volente* God willing
317	**portmanteau** clothes-hanger
322	**hypochondria** anxiety or depression
323	**blond** silk lace
324	**"with a sullen, moaning sound"** Scott, *The Lay of the Last Minstrel*, I.13.1

CRITICAL VIEWPOINT **A03**

Gayatri Spivak sees Bertha Antoinette Mason as a colonial 'other'. Within the logic of imperialism, this 'other' is seen as savage, animal-like and outlandish. Bertha's mental illness is emblematic of this – she is a distorted reflection of Jane Eyre's Englishness. According to the imperial project, Bertha Mason as a Creole must be humanised and civilised, yet this is impossible.

CHECK THE BOOK **A03**

In Jean Rhys's *Wide Sargasso Sea* a dispossessed younger son, Rochester, marries an heiress, Antoinette, purely for material gain, only then discovering the truth of rumours about the sanity of his bride and her mother. In this novel we are never entirely sure about Mrs Rochester's mental illness – it is a projection, almost an imposed charade, forced upon her by her husband. We do, however, see the English, of whom Rochester is a typical representative, exploit the resources of the Caribbean, and control the islands and their people without any cost to themselves.

CHAPTER XXVI

SUMMARY

- Jane dresses for church and Rochester hurries her on to the ceremony.

- The service begins, but as the clergyman asks if there is any impediment a man steps forward to declare that Rochester is already married, to one Bertha Antoinette Mason.

- The stranger is a solicitor and he is accompanied by Mr Mason, Mrs Rochester's brother. Mr Mason intervened as a result of Jane's letter to her uncle, Mason's employee.

- Rochester confesses his attempted bigamy and takes those in the church back to the house to meet Bertha.

- Bertha is revealed to be mentally unstable and kept under lock and key, under the care of Grace Poole.

- Jane retreats to her room.

ANALYSIS

A REVELATION

The bad omens of the last few chapters are fulfilled. Thornfield and its master's mysteries are revealed. This is the last chapter of Volume II (see **Part One: *Jane Eyre* in context**) and serves to tie up several loose ends. We are left wondering what Jane will do next.

STUDY FOCUS: MARRIAGE | A04

It is worth remembering here that the Anglican marriage service had by this point become part of the state bureaucracy, which extended across the Empire. Though the working classes continued to practise alternatives to legal marriage, illegitimate children were increasingly ostracised. Marriage was a matter of legal record and, for the elite in particular, was grounded in property relations. It was essential that a middle-class woman remained respectable – a virgin – until her wedding day. Having no property, Jane's only guarantee of a livelihood came from marriage, so her whole future, not just her moral standing, rested upon her respectability – which might in part explain Jane's rather stand-offish behaviour during her engagement. Bigamy was also taken very seriously as the woman became her husband's chattel (property) on marriage and bigamy would destroy the wife's reputation. This is why a solicitor, not simply the uncle who discovered the obstacle, comes to Jane's rescue with the declaration that 'The marriage cannot go on: I declare the existence of an impediment' (p. 333). What might have become of Jane if she had married illegally?

> **CONTEXT** | A04
>
> All marriages in England and Wales had to be registered after the Hardwicke Marriage Act of 1753. Couples planning to wed could have the banns called in the bride or groom's parish before the event, or they could obtain a licence to dispense with the banns.

GLOSSARY

337 **a Creole** a person of European and African parentage born in the West Indies, Central America, tropical South America, or the Mexican Gulf; or their descendants

339 **'Funchal correspondent of his house'** representative of the Mason firm in Funchal, capital city of Madeira

339 **'decline'** consumption

CHAPTER XXVII

SUMMARY

- Next morning Jane's conscience tells her that she must leave her employer.
- Jane is able to forgive Rochester, but though he tells her Bertha Mason's history she still refuses to become his mistress.
- That night Jane slips out, wanders over the fields and finally catches a coach that will take her away from Thornfield.

CONTEXT **A04**

Jane only has 20 shillings for the coach. Coaches could travel at up to 12 miles per hour in the 1830s, but generally stopped about every 8–10 miles, i.e. roughly one stop per hour travelled. This was a costly way to travel; the inside fare from Liverpool to Manchester was 10 shillings in 1830, while the outside fare was 6 shillings.

ANALYSIS

SYMBOLS AND MOTIFS

This chapter of heightened emotion is the last in the Thornfield section and repays close analysis. It opens with an example of **personification** in which Jane looks to her Lowood training and follows 'Conscience' not 'Passion' (p. 343). Notice how, feeling alone and unloved as she did in childhood, she recalls the red-room at Gateshead. **Symbolically** the moon is an important **motif**, while the dawn chorus that greets Jane as she leaves Thornfield reminds us of her reflections on the old chestnut tree.

ROCHESTER'S STORY

The bulk of the chapter consists of Rochester's **narrative**, through which we learn more about his character, how he has matured and his current state of mind. In contrast, the brief, **journalistic** style in which Jane's mental ordeal is described is striking. She draws on her schooling to provide her with the inner strength to tolerate extreme circumstances.

FIRE, ICE AND ROCK

The motif of fire and ice is repeated when Rochester takes Jane to a fire in the library to revive her. Her 'white cheek' contrasts with the 'hot rain of tears' (p. 344) that Rochester expected and is a sign of the extent to which she has controlled her passions, though at some cost – she 'had become icy cold' (p. 345). However, though she melts towards him and forgives him, she realises that she 'must be ice and rock to him' (p. 346).

'READER!'

Once again the reader is addressed directly at a time of crisis: 'Reader, I forgave him' (p. 344) in a way that **foreshadows** the style of 'Reader, I married him' in the final chapter of the book (p. 517). Ferndean Manor is introduced as 'even more retired and hidden than' Thornfield, in an unhealthy situation 'in the heart of a wood' with 'damp walls' (p. 347), though later it becomes Jane and Rochester's happy home.

STUDY FOCUS: MR ROCHESTER AND BERTHA MASON/ROCHESTER

A02

Rochester describes his experiences with Bertha in tones that echo Jane's own understanding of how Rochester would have changed her, Jane, in Chapter XXXI. It is suggested that Bertha's sexual excess caused her mental illness, which implies that her instability might have been caused by the final stages of syphilis rather than being genetic. Such a discussion of the cause of her mental state makes it seem quite real.

Rochester's search for the direct opposite of his wife, 'the antipodes of the Creole' (p. 358) (see **Glossary** in **Part Two: Chapter XXVI**), is in vain in part because, as he admits, he 'tried the companionship of mistresses' (p. 358), who for the Victorians would be fallen women, likened to prostitutes, the very opposite of the virginal, pure woman he says he seeks. Though she is his wife, in allowing her sexuality to reign unchecked, Bertha Mason would have been judged in a similar way. And, though Jane seems to be the opposite of Bertha, she too would become a fallen woman if Jane became Rochester's mistress. If Jane had married him at this point, do you think that the same fate – that of an imprisoned outcast – might have befallen her as an illegitimate wife?

KEY QUOTATION: CHAPTER XXVII

A01

'Terrible moment: full of struggle, blackness, burning!' (p. 363)

Possible interpretations:

- This is a pivotal moment – Jane struggles with her love for Rochester and an acute sense of what she ought to do, for propriety's sake.

- The sparseness of the language and the very vivid **imagery** – which draws on classic depictions of hell as the fiery consequence of immorality – give the reader an insight into Jane's deeply felt dilemma.

- Jane is so overwhelmed that she can barely think; reason and language begins to break down for her. In the end just 'One drear word comprised my intolerable duty – "Depart!"' (p. 363)

- The quote draws on our existing knowledge of Jane's passionate nature, which is frequently represented as fiery. The references to fire and burning also link Jane to Bertha Rochester – whose own reason has been overwhelmed by her passions, who set fire to Rochester's bedroom, and who later causes Thornfield to burn down.

CONTEXT

A04

Social commentator Harriet Martineau (1802–76) campaigned to improve the conditions under which those with mental illnesses were treated, and wrote an essay 'The Hanwell Lunatic Asylum,' *Tait's Edinburgh Magazine* (1834) on this topic, which was widely read. In it Martineau argued: 'Every one knows that it is for their own sakes that families consign an afflicted member to forgetfulness. Every one knows that the chances of recovery are incalculably lessened by the patient being withdrawn from congenial occupation and companionship.' Charlotte Brontë read and agreed with Martineau's essay.

CONTEXT

A03

Jane refers to Rochester as her 'idol' (p. 363), a word that is also picked up by Jean Rhys in *Wide Sargasso Sea*. In Part Three, Antoinette sees a clock which is made of gold and reflects 'Gold is the idol they worship.' The Bible exhorts followers to turn away from idols.

GLOSSARY

343	**'pluck out ... transfix it'**	Matthew 5:28–30
346	**'tent of Achan'**	Joshua 7
347	**upas-tree**	a poisonous tree fabled to give off a rotten vapour
347	**Grimsby Retreat**	fictional mental asylum
348	**'Samson's ... tow'**	Judges 16:9
353	**intemperate**	drinks alcohol excessively
358	**Messalina**	a woman with a heightened sexual appetite, originally the wife of the Emperor Claudius

CHAPTER XXVIII

SUMMARY

- The coach leaves Jane at Whitcross, a crossroads in the middle of the moors.
- She sleeps in a secluded spot and the next day sets out to look for work. Having no luck, she is forced to beg.
- She sleeps in a wood and the next day again fails to find work.
- Finally, Jane walks back onto the moors and discovers an isolated farmhouse. Through the window she sees an old woman, Hannah, and two young women, Diana and Mary, knitting and reading in the kitchen.
- Jane knocks. The servant refuses to help her, but just as the door is shut in her face the master, Mr St John Rivers, returns and takes her in.
- When asked her name she says she is 'Jane Elliott' (p. 387).

ANALYSIS

DESOLATION

Jane's nature will not allow her to accept her fate passively. This chapter is full of **pathos**. The language is direct, unsentimental and gives a very clear sense of the utter psychological and physical desolation that Jane feels at this point. This is made more poignant by the scene of perfect domesticity that greets her in her last desperate moments. Jane's experiences at night on the moor, where she recognises her God's 'omnipotence' and 'omnipresence' (p. 373) is comparable to **Romantic** thought about Nature's ability to teach morality, as for example in Wordsworth's *The Prelude* (published 1850).

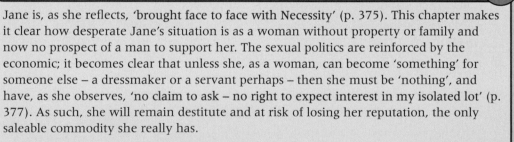

STUDY FOCUS: DESTITUTION — A02

Jane is, as she reflects, 'brought face to face with Necessity' (p. 375). This chapter makes it clear how desperate Jane's situation is as a woman without property or family and now no prospect of a man to support her. The sexual politics are reinforced by the economic; it becomes clear that unless she, as a woman, can become 'something' for someone else – a dressmaker or a servant perhaps – then she must be 'nothing', and have, as she observes, 'no claim to ask – no right to expect interest in my isolated lot' (p. 377). As such, she will remain destitute and at risk of losing her reputation, the only saleable commodity she really has.

Unable to determine her own identity, at this point, others begin conjuring up new identities for her – by the time she is finally taken in she has already been suspected of being a beggar and a criminal. In the end, though, guided by Providence, she becomes an object of charity, the best outcome that she could hope for. At which point – having become something once more – she takes back control of her character and story: 'I began' she observes 'once more to know myself' (p. 387).

GLOSSARY

382–3 **'Da trat hervor … Grimms'** quotations from Schiller, *The Robbers*, V.1

388 **'If I were a masterless … to-night'** Shakespeare, *King Lear*, IV.7.35–7

CONTEXT — A04

The New Poor Law of 1834 reformed the provision for the poor, and led to the establishment of workhouses. If people were unable to find employment or any kind of charitable relief, they had to go to the workhouses, where they lived and did menial work for a basic diet. The workhouses were feared and hated by the poor.

CRITICAL VIEWPOINT — A03

During the 1930s Lord David Cecil said of Charlotte Brontë that she 'stretches the long arm of coincidence until it becomes positively dislocated'. This oversimplifies the structure of the text, which is in fact tightly woven and very carefully crafted. As David Lodge argues, 'most of the great Victorian novelists, … wrote long, multi-stranded … stories involving numerous characters drawn from different levels of society.' In this way 'intriguing and instructive connections could be [made] between people who would not normally have had anything to do with each other.' (*The Art of Fiction* (1992), p. 150)

CHAPTER XXIX

SUMMARY

- Jane lies ill for three days but gradually recovers.
- Jane helps the servant, Hannah, and finds out more about the Rivers family and the house that they live in (known as both Moor House and Marsh End).
- Old Mr Rivers has just died and St John, Mary and Diana have come home to sort out his affairs. The sisters have been working as governesses, while St John is a clergyman.
- When the family quiz Jane about her circumstances and history, she refuses to tell them much, but does explain that she was most recently a governess.
- She asks to be called Jane Elliott, but admits that it is not her real name.
- They agree to let her stay with them until she can find some kind of employment.

ANALYSIS

JANE RECOVERS

This is a discreetly **expository** chapter in which we begin to learn something about the Rivers family. The two sisters and their brother are shown to be a family that is similar in kind, but different in character and temperament to the Reeds; they can also be read as versions of Charlotte Brontë's own family. Jane's snobbery remains intact, as revealed when she involuntarily corrects Hannah's English. From the conversation she overhears we can also see how important appearance – including the quality of one's clothing and speech – was to the Victorians in helping distinguish between who was respectable and who was not. 'Respectability' was grounded in class, as well as a person's moral conduct. The two sisters also discuss Jane's **'physiognomy'** (p. 390).

STUDY FOCUS: HOSPITALITY VS CHARITY | A03

Charlotte Brontë is critical of religion that exists only in the mind – 'if you are a Christian, you ought not to consider poverty a crime' (p. 393) – so by implication a good Christian should act charitably. However, Jane understands and insists that the Rivers's treatment of her is 'hospitality' (p. 390) – there is a further discussion of this at the end of the chapter when St John contemplates her long-term prospects. He too is 'quite sensible of the distinction' between hospitality and 'charity' (p. 400). Such a distinction was grounded in the material relations of rich and poor; the acts of giving and receiving reinforced the position of the giver and the receiver. Think about the degree to which Jane's refusal to see the Rivers's help as charity is indicative of her sense of independence, her need to maintain her self-respect, her sense of pride and her class identity.

GLOSSARY

400	**'day of small things'**	Zechariah 4:10
400	**plain-workwoman**	woman who does plain sewing

CONTEXT | A04

As a total stranger, Jane is lucky to be taken in. By the nineteenth century, 'home' was seen as a secluded haven, meant for the exclusive use of the family. Managed by the women of the household, the private sphere of the home was supposed to be a refuge from the competition and aggression of the wider world.

CHECK THE BOOK | A03

For a history of the concept of charity see Raymond Williams *Keywords: A Vocabulary of Culture and Society* (1988). There were two kinds of poor in the eyes of the Victorians: the deserving poor (who were respectable) and the undeserving poor (who were usually blamed for their plight). Only the deserving poor received charity. Many respectable working-class people saw elite charity as intrusive and having too many strings attached. Charity could therefore be seen as something that was quite distasteful.

CHAPTER XXX

SUMMARY

- Jane is very happy living with the Rivers sisters, with whom she shares tastes and interests.
- St John remains a remote figure, but he eventually asks Jane to become schoolmistress at Morton. She accepts, even though she will only teach the local cottage girls, as it will allow her to become independent.
- She also learns that the Rivers's uncle has just died and, due to a quarrel with their father, has left them out of his will. Shortly after this the sisters and their brother go their separate ways.

ANALYSIS

ST JOHN RIVERS

Though St John Rivers is an **Evangelical** clergyman he is shown to be the moral opposite of Mr Brocklehurst. Equally, compared to Rochester, St John is hard, cold and absolutely self-controlled. Even in his most passionate moments, when speaking of his faith, his cheek is 'unflushed' (p. 407). However, he is clearly displeased at the news that his uncle has left nothing to him and his sisters, apparently because he would have used it in doing good deeds. St John is quite a frightening character who can clearly overpower Jane. Jane appears uncomfortable while he discusses her new post, as he takes his time and judges her character – she dislikes the loss of control. He is so reserved that she cannot tell at first whether his dedication to the work of visiting the poor is done out of 'love or duty' (p. 404), but she can step back later and criticise his lack of human affection. Despite his philanthropic work, he seems to lack sympathy for other human beings. And it soon becomes clear that his faith is grounded in labour without rest.

STUDY FOCUS: A MAN OF FAITH — A02

St John's long-term intention, to become a missionary, is hinted at when he says of his work with the poor: 'if I let a gust of wind … turn me away from these easy tasks, what preparation would such sloth be for the future I propose to myself?' (p. 404). It is quite telling that, in speaking of himself in the third person as the last male representative of the Rivers, he 'considers himself an alien from his native country – not only in life, but in death' (p. 407). His seems to be, as with Helen Burns, a faith that looks forward to death.

CONTEXT — A04

Moor House, where the Rivers live, and its moorland location are described in detail. As well as serving literary convention, the way in which the house names in the novel reflect their locations is also typical of the area. Many working farms still bear names that refer to the original clearance of the land, the purpose of the farm or the name of the people who first farmed there, and therefore tell us something about their historic origins.

GLOSSARY

402	**enthusiasm**	fanaticism
405	**nervous**	tense and energetic
405	**election**	individual salvation
405	**peace … understanding**	Philippians 4:7
407	**Church militant**	role of the Church as the conquest of evil
407	**'Rise, follow me!'**	from the New Testament/Gospels
407	**ideal**	imaginative, opposite of material
408	**ciphering**	arithmetic
409	**'my nature … useless'**	Milton, 'When I consider …'

CHAPTER XXXI

SUMMARY

- Jane takes up her position as schoolmistress.
- As she sits in her cottage on the first evening she reflects on her actions in leaving Rochester and feels that she was right to leave him, but nonetheless is very sad.
- St John visits her and explains that he hopes to become a missionary.
- While they talk, a young lady, Miss Rosamond Oliver, the school's benefactress, arrives. There is an obvious mutual attraction between her and St John, though St John is careful not to show any expression of it.

ANALYSIS

PARALLELS

The parallels between St John and Brocklehurst continue; both men would hope to 'turn the bent of nature' (p. 416). Miss Oliver and St John are, physically, perfectly matched, like Rochester and Jane. However, St John, unlike Rochester, seems determined to turn away from love and, like Helen Burns, sacrifice himself to his faith. Indeed, **images** of death often surround him. As his sister says, and Jane concurs, St John is 'inexorable as death' (p. 421). This prefigures his death at the end of the novel.

> **CONTEXT** A04
>
> Until the Education Act 1870 there was a wide range of educational provision. The school where Jane works is a typical charity school of the period, set up with the intention of helping the poor by a local benefactress who maintains an interest in its pupils' progress.

STUDY FOCUS: THE LEGACY OF LOWOOD — A04

Jane struggles with her essential snobbishness in order to see her scholars having as much potential to learn as their social superiors. She continues to focus on her Lowood education as her beacon for good behaviour. It is her Lowood training that makes it quite clear to her that she might have become as Bertha did if she had followed her passions. As she looks at the harvest sunset, it is clear that she has reaped as she has sown.

GLOSSARY

415	**'The air … balm'**	misquotation of Sir Walter Scott's *The Lay of the Last Minstrel*, III. 14.3–4
416	**Lot's wife**	Genesis 19:26
418	**Peri**	beautiful good fairy

CHAPTER XXXII

SUMMARY

- Jane settles in at the school and becomes well liked locally, but still has disturbing dreams.
- Miss Oliver often visits the school when St John is teaching, and goes to the cottage when Jane is at home.
- Jane meets Rosamond's father, Mr Oliver, and is invited to the hall where he tells her more about the Rivers family.
- St John appears one evening while Jane is working on a sketch of Rosamond. Jane takes the opportunity to find out how he feels about Miss Oliver. Jane notices him tear a small strip from a piece of her paper.

ANALYSIS

JANE'S DREAMS

Jane's dreams provide us with a realistic picture of female desire and are notable for their psychological truth. Despite her apparent self-control, Jane is still struggling with her very real need for Rochester. The references to Rochester in the Morton section of the novel serve to link this with the Thornfield chapters and help point up the contrast between her two suitors: Rochester is all feeling, St John is all reason.

STUDY FOCUS: 'A COLD, HARD, AMBITIOUS MAN'   A02

St John is, as he says, 'a cold, hard, ambitious man' (p. 422), determined to reject life in order to build 'a mansion in heaven' (p. 431). Jane cannot understand this, but, like Helen, he lives a life of 'Christian stoicism' (p. 424) and therefore she can admire him. He shows passion when Miss Oliver is near – 'his hands would tremble and his eye burn' (p. 424) – but he resists and represses his desire. He is a 'martyr' in that he sacrifices his feelings, and seems determined to sacrifice himself for 'Paradise' (p. 424). Consider the extent to which Jane is right to question his choices, given that in the end he does wither and waste 'under a tropical sun' (p. 429).

PERIOD SETTING

The **narrator**'s brief reflections on the state of contemporary literature, which she thinks is poor compared to what she calls 'the golden age of modern literature' (p. 427) take us briefly out of the Morton episode to the narrator's own present, the age of the **Romantics** and of Sir Walter Scott's poetry.

REVISION FOCUS: TASK 3   A02

How far do you agree with the following statements?

- Jane Eyre is a reliable narrator.
- Mr Rochester and St John Rivers are opposites.

Write opening paragraphs for essays based on these discussion points. Set out your arguments clearly and ensure that your paragraphs link to each other in a logical way.

GRADE BOOSTER   A02

Look out for parallels with events beyond and within the novel. For example, Jane's deception in choosing an alias is discovered, like Guy Fawkes's plot to burn down the Houses of Parliament, on 5 November. We could argue that Jane acts devilishly in tempting St John with the painting of Miss Oliver – and then 'the original' (p. 429), i.e. Miss Oliver herself. But St John resists her, as she will resist him.

CHAPTER XXXIII

SUMMARY

- St John suddenly appears to bring Jane news.
- He recounts her own story and tells her that the strip of paper he took the day before bore her signature and confirmed her as one 'Jane Eyre' whose uncle has died and left her £20,000.
- Jane also discovers that this man is the uncle who refused to leave a penny to the Rivers family.
- Jane is an heiress and has a family.
- She decides to share the fortune with her newly identified cousins.

ANALYSIS

A FAIRY TALE ENDING BEGINS

Finally, Jane's fairy tale begins to come true. This is one of the most deliberately fantastical elements in the story, as highlighted by the fact that it takes place at Christmas, but each piece of the puzzle has been subtly introduced earlier in the novel. Jane has longed for a real home and family since the outset of the novel. She has also frequently wished to have status and to be independent, as seen when Rochester takes her shopping: 'Glad was I to get him out of the silk warehouse, and then out of a jeweller's shop: the more he bought me, the more my cheek burned with a sense of annoyance and degradation.' (Chapter XXIV, p. 309). The uncle in Madeira was introduced when she returned to Gateshead, in Chapter XXI, while the difficult relationships between the Rivers, Eyres and Reeds have been hinted at throughout. It is appropriate that Jane's real identity is revealed through her art.

STUDY FOCUS: PROPERTY   A04

Jane has become a woman of substance through the letter of the law, even though bequests and deeds normally benefit men – indeed, she can only benefit directly and choose how to dispose of her new-found wealth because she is not married. Jane, still following her Lowood schooling, takes the 'Legacy' (p. 441) quite seriously as a responsibility to be managed. This acquisition coupled with Rochester's loss of property will help to balance the material scales of class and of power in such a way as to permit their union. Consider, therefore, the way in which the inheritance begins to move the story to its conclusion.

GLOSSARY

441   **Medusa** mythological (female) creature with snake hair, to look on her is to turn to stone – she is only defeated when her opponent shows her a mirror so she gazes at her own reflection and is turned to stone

CHAPTER XXXIV

SUMMARY

- Jane shuts up the school for Christmas and goes back to Moor House.
- Diana and Mary return. St John tells them that he is determined to leave England and that Miss Oliver is to marry a Mr Granby.
- Jane is treated like a sister by Diana and Mary, but St John remains reserved. He asks her to learn Hindustani. One night he kisses her on the cheek.
- Jane wants to know what has become of Rochester and writes to Mrs Fairfax, but her letters are unanswered.
- In the summer, St John proposes; he wants a missionary's wife and thinks that Jane will be perfect. She refuses to marry him, though she says she would accompany him to India as his sister. He will not accept this offer.

> **CONTEXT**   **A04**
>
> British soldiers and administrators needed to conduct business in Indian languages, and as they would often have to learn local vernaculars, they would generally seek the aid of a *munshi* or language instructor once they arrived.

ANALYSIS

ST JOHN PROPOSES

Jane finally has a real family home to return to, something that she felt she needed when she spent time with Eliza and Georgiana in Chapter XXII, but she cannot imagine St John succumbing to domesticity and she shrinks in horror at the idea of being his wife. References to his being like stone associate him with Brocklehurst – though St John is clearly less hypocritical, he remains cold and hard. The long struggle – reflected in the length of the chapter – that now begins to take place between them is what finally brings her to maturity.

> **CONTEXT**   **A04**
>
> While proposing, St John Rivers refers to 'an East Indiaman which sails on the twentieth of June' (p. 463). Ships from the East India Company first arrived in India in 1608. The company later became a ruling, not just trading, enterprise although eventually the British government put in place a Governor-General of India. The East India Company was dissolved in 1858.

STUDY FOCUS: COLD STONE   **A02**

Jane's admiration for St John is always tempered by bleakness. She sees through his high-minded ideals, but despite this he slowly begins to overwhelm her. Her passionate nature is gradually frozen over by his kisses – the colour white clings to him as an indicator of his frigidity: 'a white stone' (p. 453) – and her observation in the next chapter that his love would kill her seems absolutely true.

GLOSSARY

451	**'confusion worse confounded'**	*Paradise Lost*, II.996
453	**Caffre**	Kaffir
455	**unlikely** (**dialect**)	unsuitable
472	**'Looked ... hill'**	Scott, *The Lay of the Last Minstrel*, V.26.1

CHAPTER XXXV

SUMMARY

- St John continues to treat Jane coolly and refuses to respond to her overtures of friendship. They fight again and when he leaves the house she explains what is going on to Diana.
- That evening, after prayers, he proposes again and she nearly succumbs.
- In a state of excitement, she begs God for help and suddenly hears Rochester's voice calling out to her.

ANALYSIS

THE REAL AND THE FANTASTIC

Through the depiction of St John, we see that in the novel unquestioning dedication to one's beliefs is seen as much worse than malicious behaviour. This radical departure from the conventions of nineteenth-century literature led to widespread criticism of the novel when it was first published. In this chapter we also see a mixture of the material world and extraordinary experience as the **narrative** moves from what is quite realistic to what is essentially supernatural.

The moment at which Jane hears Rochester's voice, we find out in the next chapter, corresponds to Rochester's own experience. However, we discover later that her hearing Rochester's voice call to her follows his recognition of 'the hand of God' (Chapter XXXVII, p. 514) in his fate. It is only after this, and once Jane recognises that her love for Rochester temporarily blinded her to God's love, that the two can be reconciled.

STUDY FOCUS: ST JOHN AND JANE **A02**

Jane sees through St John to 'the corrupt man within him' (p. 473). He is absolutely brutal in the execution of his faith and like Brocklehurst he is determined to bend Jane to his will, to kill her true self. Where Brocklehurst was 'a black pillar' (Chapter XXXV, p. 473), St John is ice-cold white 'marble' (Chapter IV, p. 38). The sheer power of St John's personality is quite terrifying and Jane's ultimate struggle with him seems to be just as dramatic as her battle with Rochester in Chapter XXVII. As she says 'I was almost as hard beset by him now as I had been once before, in a different way, by another' (p. 482). Consider the differences between Jane's battles with St John and Rochester.

CONTEXT **A02**

There is no effeminacy in St John's Christian sentiment, and he is capable of withstanding physical extremes (until he travels to India). He is rational, intelligent and determined to succeed in his missionary venture. These qualities would have led Victorians to have seen him as the epitome of manliness, yet Charlotte Brontë shows him to be engaged in a bleak and heartless quest. In this way, she questions the then dominant model of masculinity as much as she questions femininity.

JANE'S ASCENT

Whereas she venerates St John's 'talent and principle' (p. 475), and recognises that he, like Helen, is probably one of those chosen by God, her feelings for Rochester were much stronger – Rochester eclipsed her world, even her God. Therefore, to 'have yielded then [to Rochester] would have been an error of principle; to have yielded now [to St John] would have been an error of judgment' (p. 482). St John and Rochester **symbolise** the conflict between Reason and Feeling in Jane's character. Suddenly, she transcends this conflict, realises that to be herself, in order to live, she must follow her nature 'It was *my* time to assume ascendancy. *My* powers were in play and in force' (p. 484).

EXTENDED COMMENTARY

CHAPTER XXXV, PP. 482–3

From 'I stood motionless under' to '"Oh, I will come!"'

St John is as hard and 'cold as an iceberg' (Chapter XXXVII, p. 511) – in opposition to Mr Brocklehurst who is 'a black pillar' (Chapter IV, p. 38) – but in this passage he becomes gentle in an attempt to draw Jane into his plans. The setting is eerie and faintly unnatural; the room in which Jane and St John stand is dark, except for a guttering candle and the moonlight; outside all is black and silent except for the moaning March wind. It is night-time and everyone else has retired to bed. The language is **journalistic** and the tone of the piece is tense, thrilling, but quite unlike that of the garden scene in which Rochester proposed.

St John is utterly unable to bend himself to the yoke of mutual love and tenderness, and as such, is the opposite of Mr Rochester who helps Jane to the full enjoyment of life – as she herself recognises: '(… for I had felt what it was to be loved…)' (p. 482). There is no sympathy between them. St John simply tries to dominate Jane – 'He pressed his hand firmer on my head, as if he claimed me' (p. 482) – and, as we can see from the self-conscious stress on '*almost*' (p. 482), only ever gives the appearance of love. He may seem to be a high-minded clergyman, but he is actually a bully who is determined that others will submit to his will and sacrifice themselves to his cause – 'My prayers are heard!' (p. 482) he cries as she says she might marry him.

Jane has already seen through the gloss of a right-minded missionary to the ambitious man within – 'I should not the less be made to repent, some day, of my former rebellion' (p. 482) but she still finds it hard to withstand his assaults on her own hard-won identity. This is because she wants to do what is morally right. Through St John and Jane's relationship Charlotte Brontë exposes the Victorian myth of self-denying **asceticism** which, juxtaposed against a real and deeply felt morality that has nothing to do with social convention, is shown to equate with the heartless sacrifice of others.

CONTEXT **A03**

Nineteenth-century stage adaptations tended to tame and domesticate Jane, presumably finding her too subversive. She had to be represented either as a good moral woman or as a selfish and wilful one; it was difficult for her to be seen as both virtuous and strong-minded at this time.

Where Rochester tempted Jane to throw away social convention and duty, so St John tempts her to throw away her passion, to renounce her nature entirely. And because fate has brought them together she finds it hard to see clearly whether or not she should marry him – 'I contended with my inward dimness of vision, before which clouds yet rolled' (pp. 482–3). However, Rochester's love is transcendent. And, as Jane cries to heaven for help, so she receives her aid and escapes St John's bleak vision of faith. Where Rochester called out to God to sanction the bigamous marriage, St John calls on God to support his own shallow and essentially meaningless proposal. Where Providence previously spoke through the destruction of the chestnut tree, this time Jane hears Rochester's voice, which both Rochester and Jane interpret, independently, as a manifestation of God's will. It is only after both recognise the necessity of God's intervention that they may finally come together and marry.

CONTEXT **A04**

Bigamy, along with illegitimacy and adultery, became a staple plot device in the Sensation Novels of the 1860s. Sensation Novels, such as Mary Braddon's *Lady Audley's Secret* (1862), could be highly subversive and were enormously popular. They were not treated as having literary merit in their day, but there was debate about their corrupting influence on the public taste.

CHAPTER XXXVI

SUMMARY

- The next day Jane catches the coach to Thornfield. She walks the final two miles across the fields to the Hall.

- When she reaches it she sees nothing but a burnt-out shell.

- On asking at The Rochester Arms she discovers that there has been a fire, that Bertha is dead and that Mr Rochester is alive, but was injured when he tried to save her.

- Rochester is now living at Ferndean and Jane organises a carriage to take her there.

ANALYSIS

JANE'S RETURN TO THORNFIELD

As we reach the **denouement** so the tension mounts. Jane's departure from Morton echoes her flight from Thornfield a year earlier; but now she is absolutely sure of herself and her actions, though she has no way of guessing the consequences. She has become a mature woman who knows her own mind and can resist convention.

MATERIAL WEALTH

Jane also has the money to complete two journeys, not just one, to destinations of her choosing. And she is quite conscious of this: on stepping into the coach at Whitcross, she reflects: 'I entered – not now obliged to part with my whole fortune as the price of its accommodation' (p. 487). In Chapter XXXVII she makes the point that she dismisses 'the chaise and driver with the double remuneration I had promised' (p. 497). The material conditions that impact on Jane's situation – which are part of the sexual politics of the day – are stated as clearly as the ideas of the time that affect her.

STUDY FOCUS: SYMPATHIES OF PLACE AND CHARACTER A02

Jane's dream, in Chapter XXV, foretold that the hall would be burnt down. But its destruction is especially shocking to her as she associates the place with the figure of its, and her, 'master': she observes that the landscape around Thornfield 'met my eye like the lineaments of a once familiar face' (p. 487). In looking at Thornfield Hall itself, she then uses the **analogy** of a lover anticipating gazing upon the face of 'his mistress' (p. 489) as she sleeps only to find her lying dead. Later, of course, we find that Rochester like Thornfield has been scarred by fire. Further links to previous chapters possibly include the fact that it burned down 'just about harvest-time' (p. 491) a time when in Chapter XXXI Jane had been gazing out across the fields from her new cottage home and struggling with regret.

SERVANTS

There's a shrewd and accurate observation from the old butler, in reporting the tale of the hall, that the servants 'used to watch him – servants will, you know' (p. 492). This might be a rather wry comment on Charlotte Brontë's part, as it represents how Jane herself construed much of her **narrative** – and on hearing her story retold in part somewhat differently by the old man, Jane becomes, as ever when the story moves beyond her control, a little irritable.

KEY QUOTATION: CHAPTER XXXVI A01

'I witnessed, and several more witnessed, Mr Rochester ascend through the sky-light on to the roof; we heard him call "Bertha!" We saw him approach her; and then, ma'am, she yelled and gave a spring, and the next moment she lay smashed on the pavement.' (p. 493)

Possible interpretations:

- It is crucial that there are several witnesses to testify that Rochester went to his wife's aid, and that she leapt to her death – this guarantees that Rochester no longer has a wife, that her death was accidental and that he has been a good husband.

- The **imagery** surrounding Bertha Rochester in this passage confirms that she is mad, in Victorian eyes. In the use of 'yelled' (p. 493) we are given to believe that she is beyond language and therefore beyond reason, and in the word 'spring' (p. 493) she becomes animalistic.

CRITICAL VIEWPOINT A04

Charlotte Brontë wrote of her depiction of Bertha after publication: 'I agree … that the character is shocking … It is true that profound pity ought to be the only sentiment elicited by the view of such degradation, and equally true that I have not sufficiently dwelt on that feeling; I have erred in making *horror* too predominant.' (Peter Grudin, 'Jane and the Other Mrs. Rochester' in *Novel: A Forum on Fiction* (1977), cited by D. Christopher Gabbard, 'From Custodial Care to Caring Labour', in David Bolt, Julia Miele Rodas & Elizabeth J. Donaldson, *The Madwoman and the Blindman; Jane Eyre discourse, disability* (2012), p. 101n5).

GLOSSARY

485	**'watch and pray … weak'**	Matthew 36:41, Mark 14:38
486	**like the earthquake … aghast**	Acts 16:26–9
488	**tideless sea of the South**	Mediterranean

CHAPTER XXXVII

SUMMARY

- Jane reaches Ferndean as night falls and sees Rochester in the yard. She realises that he has lost his sight and damaged his arm.
- She goes in and introduces herself to John and Mary, the servants, then takes Rochester candles and a glass of water, pretending to be the maid.
- Their reunion is emotional and joyful.
- They eat supper together and the next morning she explains what she has been doing.
- We learn that Rochester called to Jane, and when she cried out in return he heard her. Rochester has learned to put his fate in God's hands and believes that this has facilitated their union.
- Eventually he proposes for the second time and she accepts.

ANALYSIS

FERNDEAN

There is a little **exposition** at the beginning of the chapter as Ferndean Manor is introduced as 'a building of considerable antiquity, moderate size, and no architectural pretensions, deep buried in a wood' (p. 496). But, the language is fluid, the conversation natural. Once inside the bounds of Ferndean, its surrounding trees effectively entrap Jane – it is dusk and she is entering a strange sylvan (wooded) world, which is slightly **Gothic** and echoes Thornfield and the woodland in Shakespeare's *A Midsummer Night's Dream*. The lack of a feminine influence is suggested by the fact that there are 'no flowers, no garden-beds' (p. 497). The trees, the path, the railing, the gravel walk that encloses the ground, the portal, together make up a processional of privacy that she only gradually accesses. The repelling architecture of the building – its front-facing 'pointed gables', its 'narrow' 'latticed' windows and 'narrow' door (p. 497) – reflects the newly inward-looking and defensive character of its master.

STUDY FOCUS: ROCHESTER AND EYRE IN BALANCE **A04**

This is a magical chapter in which Jane and Rochester slip easily into their old ways – she teases him for a while to make him jealous then soothes him again – but in which they are both altered. Jane and Rochester have both matured. Rochester has learnt to respect Jane – his realisation at their initial meeting that 'I must be aided, and by that hand' (p. 360) comes true – while she has learnt to care for him, but also to act according to her nature. It has been argued that Rochester's loss of property and his injuries have in a sense 'feminised' him. It is this, aside from the convenience of losing his first wife who had been the literal legal impediment to his and Jane's marriage, that facilitates their coming together. With this and the fact that Jane has risen in the world – via a (normally masculine) stroke of luck in her inheritance – their relative social positions, and their gendered positions, have balanced out. Do you agree?

GLOSSARY

498	**sightless Samson** Samson's eyes are put out when he is betrayed (Judges 16:21)
505	**'to leave my tale half told'** this is what Scheherazade does in order to avoid execution in the *Arabian Nights*

CRITICAL VIEWPOINT **A02**

The name 'Ferndean' is much softer and more enclosing than the open and prickly 'Thornfield'.

CONTEXT **A04**

Rochester's withdrawal to Ferndean and the happy life they end up leading there is a little odd given what he says about it in Chapter XXVII and Jane's description of it, which confirms what he has said. Its 'ineligible and insalubrious site' (p. 496) marks Ferndean as unrentable. This is due to the widespread opinion that houses must have fresh air flowing through and around them to avoid the pitfalls of disease thought to be spread in bad air. A wooded position might be picturesque, but it was not considered healthy.

CHAPTER XXXVIII

SUMMARY

- 'Reader, I married him' (p. 517): Jane and Rochester marry quietly.
- She writes to Mary, Diana and St John; later, both Diana and Mary marry.
- She visits Adèle and moves her from one school to another; over time the girl grows up into a pleasant young woman.
- Jane and Rochester are very happy together; his sight partially recovers and they have a son.
- St John Rivers never marries; at the close of the novel he is waiting to die in India.

ANALYSIS

LOOSE ENDS

In this final chapter various loose ends are tied up. The **narrator** tells us what has happened to each of the key characters and links are made back across the novel – for instance we learn that Adèle has been sent to school, but that this, much like Lowood perhaps, is too strict, so Jane finds her another. Jane's prejudices – or rather those of her class and time – can be seen again in her comment that Adèle's 'sound English education corrected in a great measure her French defects' (p. 519).

STUDY FOCUS: 'READER, I MARRIED HIM' **A02**

Rochester and Jane have established a relationship based on mutual dependence. However, it is worth noting that Jane says 'Reader, I married him' (p. 517), not 'we were married'. It is only after Jane's powers have been established for some time that Rochester begins to regain his sight. Also, the novel does not end with Jane's description of her married bliss, but with St John's imminent death. This leads us to consider whether or not this is a conventional happy ending.

IS *JANE EYRE* A ROMANCE?

If we read the novel as a love story then this ending might surprise us, but if we read it as a text that deals primarily with issues of religion and sensibility, or even simply as a confessional **Bildungsroman**, then Jane's reflective tone becomes easier to understand. She has become a complex person; sincere yet able to question Christian doctrine and social mores, an individual who is aware of the impact of her actions on others, energetic, contemplative and self-determined, ruled in equal measure by reason and passion.

> **CRITICAL VIEWPOINT** **A03**
>
> John Mackenzie argued in his 'Imperialist Texts and the Environment' paper given at Bath in 1998 that in the nineteenth century the Empire was seen as a chaotic environment that needed ordering. This ordering happened literally, via surveying and mapping of places, but also more indirectly through the mapping of diseases, management of forests, creation of bureaucratic systems, design of cities, churches, railway stations and houses.

GLOSSARY

518	**'who live without God ... things'**	Philippians 3:19
519	**bone of ... flesh**	Genesis 2:23
521	**Greatheart**	character from Bunyan's *The Pilgrim's Progress*, who escorts women and children
521	**'without fault ... God'**	Revelation 14:5
521	**'incorruptible crown'**	I Corinthians 9:25
521	**'His own words ... this'**	Revelation 22:20

CHARACTERS

JANE EYRE

WHO IS JANE EYRE?

- Jane Eyre is a poor girl who grows up with her wealthy aunt and cousins at Gateshead.
- She is sent away to Lowood school.
- Jane is employed as a governess at Thornfield Hall, and falls passionately in love with her employer, Mr Rochester.
- Mr Rochester proposes marriage, but on their wedding day it is revealed that he already has a wife, and Jane runs away.
- She is taken in by the Rivers family, whom she later finds are her cousins.
- Jane inherits a fortune.
- St John Rivers proposes marriage, but Jane refuses him.
- Jane returns to Thornfield to find that it has burned down, and Rochester's first wife has died.
- Jane Eyre marries Mr Rochester and they have a son.

JANE'S DEVELOPMENT

At the beginning of the novel Jane is angry, rebellious and hungry for adventure, but as she grows up she learns how to temper her wilder passions so that, unlike many characters in Victorian novels, she is not destroyed by them. Her feelings, especially 'Conscience' and 'Passion' (Chapter XXVII, p. 343), are often given voices of their own when she is suffering some particular anguish and these moments of **personification** help us to

understand why she acts as she does. Torn throughout the novel between her true nature and social convention, in the end she is able to resolve this inherent division by marrying for duty and for love. Yet that victory is one that she can only achieve, as in a fairy tale, by apparent coincidence, or good luck.

JANE'S PLACE

Jane Eyre is essentially a young woman who is trying to grow up in a society that does not value her or her skills; she is an outsider. Ultimately she asserts herself, liberates herself and makes herself happy because she believes she has a right to be so. Though impoverished, she can be quite a snob and has to learn that the poor are not just an amorphous mass. As an adult, she is also imbued with the idea that everything foreign is intrinsically unhealthy and immoral. She makes sure that little Adèle learns to be English, or at least as English as possible, given that she is a French Catholic, and she assumes that the Indian climate will kill her. These are the attitudes of her time and of her class.

GRADE BOOSTER **A02**

Consider how the form of the novel shapes its meaning. Jane is Cinderella-like, or like the heroine of 'The Beauty and the Beast' or 'Bluebeard', so you could argue that it is the complex psychic development that she undergoes and the everyday setting of the novel that manage to make her such an impressive character, rather than her somewhat implausible story.

STUDY FOCUS: IS JANE A RELIABLE NARRATOR? A02

Jane dominates and controls the **narrative** – incidentally, remember that a first-person narrator is not the author, despite the novel's original subtitle, 'An Autobiography' – and her reactions and feelings always form the focus of attention, even when another character is talking about him or herself. Jane is a credible and realistic character, and because we are privy to her innermost thoughts, we generally take her to be a reliable observer. But, it is important to remember that Jane is narrating events ten years after her marriage. Though she is a child at Gateshead, she tells us about this period as a mature woman, and she herself reminds us of this. Should we question her story at all?

KEY QUOTATIONS: JANE A01

Key quotation 1:

As Mr Rochester's servants comment at Ferndean in the *Conclusion*, 'If she ben't one o' th' handsomest, … i' his een she's fair beautiful, onybody may see that.' (p. 518).

Possible interpretations:

● Jane is plain both as a child and as an adult.

● True love transforms the adored person: Edward Rochester sees Jane with his heart.

● Servants see and hear all – here they add credibility to Jane's narrative, though it is she who reports what she overhears.

Key quotation 2:

The last chapter of the novel provides a summary of Jane and Edward Rochester's life together. Its first line is: 'Reader, I married him.' (p. 517).

Possible interpretations:

● This sparse sentence brings the novel to its fairy-tale conclusion.

● The sharp, reductive language reflects both the simplicity of Jane's feelings about the event and their power. Her most deeply felt emotions are always conveyed in the most minimal terms.

● This is an astonishing statement, even though it fulfils both the **protagonist**'s and the reader's hopes, as becomes clearer when Jane describes her passing on the news to Mr Rochester's servants.

CRITICAL VIEWPOINT A02

The heart of the novel lies in Jane's descriptions of what is going on in her own mind – we are privy to her innermost thoughts and deepest feelings – and we are therefore drawn into a very close relationship with her. She is not, however, a wholly sympathetic figure.

MR ROCHESTER

WHO IS MR ROCHESTER?

- Edward Rochester is the Master of Thornfield Hall; he inherited the estate from his brother, but was a wild young man before this.
- He is the husband of Bertha (Mason) Rochester, who he keeps locked in the attic at Thornfield.
- He is the guardian of a young French girl, Adèle, possibly his daughter, and he employs Jane Eyre to be her governess.
- Rochester falls passionately in love with Jane Eyre, and tries to marry her bigamously.
- He seeks to save Bertha from a fire which devastates Thornfield – he fails, and is badly hurt in the process.
- Rochester marries Jane and they have a son.

A BYRONIC HERO

Mr Rochester's growth is important to the unfolding of the plot but, as a secondary character, he is slightly less convincing than Jane Eyre. His story is one of sin and redemption and he is a **Romantic** figure who is well bred, with brooding, rugged good looks, and combines masculine strength with tenderness. Forceful, passionate and independent, he is determined initially to have Jane, either as his wife or as his mistress, whatever the cost. Rochester never tries to woo Jane on bended knee. He often refers to her as a bird, fairy, a sprite and an imp, and he does not idealise her. She can always match him blow for blow when they argue, and their witty banter brings both characters alive and develops their mutual respect. The courtship scenes present us with a remarkable departure from literary convention.

OPPOSITIONS

Rochester is **symbolic** of the part of Jane that is fiery and passionate, rather than icy and self-controlled. As such he is also St John Rivers's opposite. Rochester is heavy and dark, whereas St John is handsome and fair; Rochester is a man of passion and fire, whereas St John is ambitious, hard and cold. Where Rochester brings Jane alive, she finds St John's passion quite deadly. The two men act as **foils** for each other.

CRITICAL VIEWPOINT **A02**

Rochester eventually learns that he must depend on, respect and see Jane as an individual if he is to win her hand. This outcome is **foreshadowed** by their first meeting, when his horse falls in the road and he has to lean on her in order to get back to his horse. In the end, his dependence on her is made more concrete by his blindness – at which point she loves him more than when he tried to protect her or shower her with gifts.

STUDY FOCUS: DISABILITY

A02

One reading would see Rochester's disability as enabling Jane to combine passion with duty. Yet, this ending is also unconventional because, though Rochester ultimately regains the sight in one eye, Jane marries him before this happens, and he remains an amputee. So, although his disability may adhere to the Victorian convention of the 'school of pain', the fact that he is not fully cured following his redemption may not. (See **Disability** in **Part Five: Critical debates**.)

KEY QUOTATIONS: ROCHESTER

A01

Key quotation 1:

In Chapter XIV Rochester speaks to Jane: '"I know what my aim is, what my motives are; and at this moment I pass a law, … that both are right. … though they absolutely require a new statute: unheard-of combinations of circumstances demand unheard-of rules." "That sounds a dangerous maxim, sir;"' (p. 161)

Possible interpretations:

- Rochester has fallen, or is falling, in love with Jane and contemplating the impossibility of his situation as a married man. He wishes that he could alter his circumstances legally. But, he will make up his own laws if needs be.
- Jane's response signals that what he seeks is both socially and morally wrong, even though she does not know what it is.
- This also **foreshadows** Jane's response to his eventual proposal that she become his mistress, which indicates that she will always adhere to what is right, even if she wishes circumstances were otherwise.

Key quotation 2:

Jane says in the final chapter of the novel 'To be together is for us to be at once as free as in solitude, as gay as in company. … to talk to each other is but a more animated and audible thinking' (p. 519).

Possible interpretations:

- Rochester and Jane's relationship is one that eventually results in a marriage of equals.
- We do not generally know Rochester's innermost thoughts because Jane does not know them. We know him as she knows him: through conversation.

> **CONTEXT** **A04**
>
> A legally separated wife could not keep her own earnings until the Matrimonial Causes Act of 1857. Married women did not receive the same rights over their property – including wages and inheritance – as single women until the Married Woman's Property Act in 1882.

St John Rivers

Who is St John Rivers?

- St John Rivers is a clergyman who lives with his two sisters, Diana and Mary, in an isolated country parish.

- He and his sisters turn out to be Jane's cousins.

- He hopes to become a missionary to India, but in the meantime does all he can to follow his calling.

- He proposes to Jane because he would like her to help him in his mission, though in fact he loves Miss Rosamond Oliver 'wildly' (p. 431). Jane turns him down.

Faith

St John Rivers is not a sympathetic character, but he is reliable – he is quite honest about his limitations – and convincing. St John always acts consistently if unnaturally, as suggested by the fact that he will not follow his nature and marry the woman he loves. His faith, like that of Helen Burns, is one that is grounded in self-sacrifice. At the conclusion of the novel, we learn that like Helen Burns he is about to die in consummation of his faith, and this makes Jane cry. His path has led to death, whereas her path has led to life-giving happiness.

CHECK THE BOOK **A03**

In Emily Brontë's *Wuthering Heights* (1847), the heroine, Catherine, is torn between two very different suitors: the violently passionate Heathcliff and the gentle Edgar Linton. This can be seen as a parallel with the choice Jane must make between Mr Rochester and St John Rivers. While Catherine's love for Heathcliff ends in tragedy, however, Jane follows her heart and finds her happy ending. Consider the similarities and differences between the fate of the heroines in these two novels.

STUDY FOCUS: ONE HALF OF JANE? **A02**

St John **symbolises** that side of Jane's character which wishes to conform, to obey the rules and suppress her instincts. Jane recognises that if she accepts him as her husband she will be crushed, she will lose her identity just as surely as if she had become Rochester's mistress. Both men represent only one half of her and this is why she runs away from St John, back to Thornfield. It is worth considering, however, the fact that the final passages in the novel are nevertheless devoted to St John.

KEY QUOTATION: ST JOHN RIVERS **A01**

In making plans to go to India, St John teaches Jane Hindustani, and subsequently proposes: '"Jane, come with me to India: come as my helpmeet and fellow-labourer … God and nature intended you for a missionary's wife. … you are formed for labour, not for love."' (p. 464)

Possible interpretations:

- St John wants Jane to join him, believing her physically and mentally formed for the task. He admires her intellect and her character, but will never love her.

- He believes that it is God's will that she become his wife, and cannot credit her refusal. It would have been conventional and appropriate in the eyes of Victorian readers for her to accept.

- When he proposes again, Jane almost succumbs to his will, but hears Rochester's voice when she seeks a sign.

MINOR CHARACTERS

BESSIE

Jane wins her first moral victory over the nursemaid Bessie who, though she is a relatively minor character, reappears several times – at Lowood and when Jane returns to Gateshead – thus providing a link between the earlier and later parts of the novel. Bessie's ballads and **folklore** stay with Jane throughout the text, and because Bessie is the only real figure of ordinary, unrefined human kindness in the book she is one of the most sympathetic characters we meet.

THE REEDS

The Reed family, on the other hand, are utterly detestable characters. They treat Jane as a nobody, and because we see them entirely from Jane's point of view it is hard to see any good in them. Mrs Reed hates Jane because she has been foisted upon them and Jane's cousins, John, Eliza and Georgiana, take their lead from their mother. By treating Jane so badly, Mrs Reed knows that she is not obeying her husband's last wish and therefore feels a certain amount of guilt. She deals with this by sending Jane away. The Reeds show us how Jane is a social outcast and her response to them demonstrates how she blankly refuses to accept her lot.

THE RIVERS

The Rivers family present us with a reminder of and a contrast with the Reed family. Unlike the Reeds, the Rivers family offer Jane genuine help when they take her in. Where the two Reed sisters, Eliza and Georgiana, represent two extremes of femininity that are equally despicable, the two Rivers sisters, Diana and Mary, are ideal women and become Jane's role models. Where her cousin John Reed was physically violent towards her, her cousin St John Rivers becomes her teacher.

CONTEXT A03

The Rivers family were reputedly modelled closely on Charlotte Brontë's own sisters and brother, though in idealised form.

MR BROCKLEHURST

Just before Jane leaves Gateshead Mrs Reed introduces her to the proprietor of Lowood school, Mr Brocklehurst. At Lowood school Jane faces the same treatment as she received at Gateshead, but on a larger scale and in a religious community. Both Gateshead and Lowood work as models of Victorian society, but Brocklehurst in particular represents a form of religious doctrine that Jane instinctively rejects. His faith is all 'hell-fire and brimstone'; he oppresses the children under his care with an extreme **Evangelical** zeal.

At one point Brocklehurst picks on a girl, Julia Severn, who has curly red hair, simply because he assumes that she must have curled it out of vanity. When he is told that her curls are natural he then insists that they be cut off because the children should not conform to nature. The next moment his own daughters appear, dressed in fine clothes and wearing their hair according to the latest fashion. This certainly indicates that his religious principles are a mockery of Christianity and that he is a hypocrite who cannot act consistently, but it also suggests that anyone who deviates from the hypocritical standards he sets will be cut out like a canker. He is an example of the men who held power in Victorian Britain and the message is that when men like Brocklehurst hold the reins, there is no way to live and be yourself; anyone who fails to conform will be pushed out of the way.

HELEN BURNS

At Lowood, Jane is not simply subject to Brocklehurst's rule, but also makes friends with Helen Burns who, in sharp contrast to Brocklehurst, represents an ideal of Christian practice. Helen's initial interest in Samuel Johnson's work *Rasselas* tells the reader everything we need to know about her. This book argues that only surrender and self-control will enable one to bear the difficulties of life; Helen endures this world simply because she, like St John, can look forward to the joys of the next. For instance, Helen is singled out by one of the teachers, but always turns the other cheek and, as an ideal Christian woman of the period, meekly resigns herself to her fate.

MISS TEMPLE

When Helen dies Jane soon rejects her bleak vision of self-sacrifice, and quickly falls under the perfect Miss Temple's spell. Miss Temple, Jane's teacher, also has to conform. When she follows her best instincts and gives the children an extra lunch because they have missed breakfast, we are quite clear that she is in the right, but she dare not talk back to Mr Brocklehurst when he upbraids her for her simple kindness. Miss Temple's self-control is a model for Jane until her mentor leaves the school, at which point her effect on Jane begins to fade. Through her friendship with Helen and Miss Temple, Jane learns the sacrifices demanded of women and, once she is beyond their influence, quickly looks for an alternative.

MRS ROCHESTER

Mrs Rochester, in her complete rejection of self-control, can be seen as an alternative to the Victorian ideal of femininity. We can see Bertha as Jane Eyre's alter ego, that side of Jane that is driven entirely by passion. She is Rochester's wife, the role promised to Jane, but which she prevents Jane from taking up, as **symbolised** by her destruction of Jane's veil on the night before her wedding day. Whereas Bertha as an outcast is powerless, Jane has some control over her life, and a renewed adoption of the values embodied by Helen and Miss Temple allows her to escape Bertha's fate. If Jane had followed her heart's desire and stayed with Rochester at this point, she would in a sense have become another Bertha, another so-called 'madwoman' driven purely by her appetites. Luckily, of course, Bertha's final act means that Jane can ultimately resolve the opposition in herself between passion and self-control.

CONTEXT **A04**

Bertha is described as a 'Creole' (Chapter XXVI, p. 337). Today 'Creole' refers to a language, combining African and French languages, and to French and Spanish settlers in the southern United States especially in and around Louisiana, but then it also meant someone born of African and French, or African and Spanish, ancestry.

MISS INGRAM, MISS OLIVER AND MRS FAIRFAX

These three women, because they are simply **foils** for the other characters, remain relatively two-dimensional and seem in effect to be cast aside once their job is done. Rochester uses Blanche Ingram in order to discover Jane's feelings and once he is finished with the heiress we hear no more about her – unusually, we do not even know if she finally marries.

Miss Rosamond Oliver, in direct contrast to Jane, is both moneyed and beautiful. An 'earthly angel' (Chapter XXXI, p. 418) she is the perfect match for St John Rivers who loves her but spurns her because he knows that she would not make a good missionary's wife. This is when Jane and the reader come to realise that St John is both indefatigable and entirely capable of suppressing his own feelings in the service of his God.

Mrs Fairfax, the housekeeper, is a distant relative of Mr Rochester's who, like Jane, is poor but genteel. Where Jane's father was a clergyman, Mrs Fairfax was married to one. She shows Jane, and therefore the reader too, around Thornfield and provides information about the locality and people, including its master. Unlike Jane, however, Mrs Fairfax is not a great observer of character and takes a back seat soon after Jane meets Rochester. Mrs Fairfax then hovers in the background as a moral bystander until Jane leaves Thornfield. When Jane returns we learn that the housekeeper has been sent away to her friends with a handsome annuity.

CONTEXT **A04**

To become a housekeeper a woman would normally work her way up through the servant ranks, from scullery-maid onwards. A housekeeper was the highest-ranking female servant in the household and answered directly to the mistress, where there was one.

STUDY FOCUS: MARRIAGES A02

Miss Temple marries a clergyman, described by Jane as 'almost worthy of such a wife' (p. 100). Miss Oliver does not marry her first choice, St John Rivers, instead getting engaged to the wealthy Mr Granby. Georgiana is described as making 'an advantageous match with a wealthy, worn-out man of fashion' (p. 279).

Only two women seem to achieve companionate marriages like Jane's: Diana and Mary Reed. Diana Reed's husband Captain Fitzjames, seems to be a good choice, being described as 'a captain in the navy, a gallant officer, and a good man' (p. 520). Likewise, Mary also seems to do well by marrying a friend of her brother's: Mr Wharton, 'a clergyman, … and, from his attainments and principles, worthy of the connection' (p. 520).

KEY QUOTATIONS: MINOR CHARACTERS A01

Key quotation 1: Blanche Ingram

Miss Blanche Ingram is described by Rochester as '"A strapper – a real strapper, … big, brown, and buxom"' (Chapter XX, p. 253)

Possible interpretations:

- There is some ambiguity in Rochester's description of Miss Ingram when talking to Jane. Miss Ingram looks just like Bertha Antoinette Mason – and in many respects also behaves like her – before Bertha married Edward. But, Rochester could also be talking about Bertha, whom Jane has seen the night before this conversation takes place.
- Whereas, as a gentlewoman, Miss Ingram might be expected to represent the Victorian ideal of femininity – delicate, slight, white and sexless – this description places her on the wrong side of the racial and sexual binary of Self and Other.

Key quotation 2: Rosamond Oliver

The last we hear about Rosamond is that she '"is about to be married to Mr Granby, one of the best connected and most estimable residents in S–"' (Chapter XXXIV, p. 456).

Possible interpretations:

- St John sees this as a victory as he has avoided temptation, but it is one that Jane sees as too costly as he has missed out on the chance to love.
- The marriage Rosamond makes is conventional and appropriate for a woman of her standing. It secures her reputation and future, and is of a type to which the other single elite women in the novel generally aspire.

CONTEXT A04

As Edward Said explains in *Orientalism*, 'race' in the nineteenth century was thought of in terms of a series of binary oppositions between good and bad. Those on the 'good' side were seen as being superior to those on the 'bad'. For the Victorians, this was also true of male/female. There was a clear division between the supposed ideal (the Self) and its supposed opposite (the Other).

THEMES

GROWING UP

The central theme of the novel is explored
through one young woman's attempt to grow up
and gain respect in a society that does not value
her or her talents. The problem of being a woman
in early Victorian Britain is the key to our
understanding of the text. To begin with, at
Gateshead, Jane learns that moral courage can
give her the power to withstand moral
oppression. Because of this she is able to make
friends with Bessie and dominate Aunt Reed. As
she enters Lowood, however, she is again
exposed to injustice and encounters two new
ways of dealing with this, first in the form of stoic
Christian forgiveness and meekness, as embodied

in Helen Burns, and second, submission to social custom, as embodied in Miss Temple. She
takes both on board for a while, but neither seems to satisfy her. She discovers that she
must be true to herself and that to achieve this she must become independent.

SEARCH FOR IDENTITY

Jane's search for identity takes her to Thornfield where
she finds some happiness, but where she is still restless
until the master of the house appears. After she follows
her deepest desires and accepts Rochester's proposal she
becomes acutely sensitive to signs of ill-fortune and is all
too aware of the bad omens that surround their future
marriage. She is still caught off guard, however, when the
final calamity falls and she has to deal with the
consequences of her actions. On discovering that
Rochester is already married, she acts entirely according
to convention, as learned at Lowood, by fleeing
Thornfield in order to regain some self-control. She does
not succumb to passion because her education has shown
her that passion is not a fit motive for action. If she lived
with Rochester she would be a social outcast and lose her
partial and hard-won independence.

SELF-FULFILMENT

For a while, this seems to have been the right move. After the Rivers family rescue her, she
finds all that she ever wanted: money, status, a family, a home. Hard work and a sound
morality seem to bring their own reward. However, as St John Rivers asks her to marry
him simply for form's sake and to become a missionary's wife, she rediscovers her true self.
She finds that she cannot completely abandon her passions after all. It is only when she
returns to Rochester, having matured and learnt the necessity of combining desire with
duty, that she can live happily ever after. The novel is therefore about women's intellectual
and emotional needs, the search for identity, and the way in which passion has to be
reconciled with self-control. The events that shape the novel test Jane and give the reader
the opportunity to explore her deepest motivations and feelings. The plot, characters and
language all form an exploration of the theme, but, to a large extent in this instance, the
theme actually dictates the form.

CONTEXT **A04**

It was still being said in
1880 that the 'missionary
and educational work in
India, China ... and other
parts of the world, offers
a vast and most
interesting field to
young women of
intelligence, earnest
religious opinions, and
some enterprise, who
have few home ties, and
are quick at adapting
themselves to new
conditions of life.'
('Occupations Accessible
to Women. III. Posts of
Superintendence',
Cassells Household Guide,
Cassell, London
(c.1880s), p. 174.)

STUDY FOCUS: THE NECESSITY OF MARRIAGE **A04**

The novel suggests that it is not enough for a woman simply to be respectable or independent. No matter how rewarding it is for an unmarried woman to make a success of her life through quiet perseverance and a clear moral stand, the implication is that it is better if she can share her life with an equal, someone who is a companion who will support her and whom she can support in turn. The novel ends with a marriage of equals. Is Rochester's development important in helping Jane complete her own growth?

CONTEXT **A04**

The distinctions between classes could be quite subtle, and class might be best thought of in this period in terms of the relationships involved, for example, the sense of identification with one class or another, rather than as something based purely on income or employment.

SOCIAL CLASS

Another, less obvious, theme tackles the much broader problem of social class. Though on one level the novel is a love story which covers the experiences of one woman, a representative of her sex, it also deals with the difficulties faced by a particular class of women in Victorian society: young middle-class women – especially governesses – who were underprivileged. Interestingly, the novel does not really provide these women with a radical solution to their problems.

Though Jane makes a success of her own life, through sheer force of will coupled with a lucky inheritance, she does not offer a way out for those middle-class women who remained in reduced circumstances, or for those who wanted to break the bounds of social convention. She does not save Helen Burns, for instance, whose tendency to self-sacrifice leads to her eventual death, or Eliza Reed who ends up, unsatisfactorily as far as Jane is concerned, in a convent. Most of the other women from her class – including Miss Temple, Miss Oliver and Georgiana Reed – marry according to the prevailing custom of the day by making slightly compromising matches, and we do not even know what happens to others – Miss Ingram, for instance, vanishes without trace.

THE MARRIAGE MARKET

As well as being a governess, Jane (like Charlotte Brontë) was the daughter of a clergyman. Clergymen held a peculiarly ambivalent position in English society, being well educated, having high aspirations, often being the younger sons of 'good families', but not being wealthy. As a consequence, the daughters of clergymen, while frequently mixing with the upper classes, would not have been countenanced as potential spouses, either by the upper classes or often even by the middle classes, as they brought no dowry with them. This is why – on a more mundane level – one of the themes of the novel is therefore the 'marriage market'. In this respect the book ends happily because the 'good' win out and find husbands: Jane does, and so do Diana and Mary, Miss Temple and Miss Oliver.

STUDY FOCUS: MONEY　　A04

In Victorian England, in order to make a good match a would-be bride needed to have money. It is money that motivates Mr Rochester to marry Bertha, a foreigner whom he hardly knew – he was offered a large sum of money to do so. This is also why it is so seemingly remarkable that Mr Rochester first proposes to Jane and rejects Miss Ingram. **Ironically**, he only legitimately proposes to Jane after their discussion of her inheritance. Note also that after Jane inherits she is deemed by St John to be a fitting spouse and that Diana and Mary are able to marry once Jane has handed over part of her fortune. Think about the part that money plays throughout the novel.

CONTEXT　　A04

Charlotte Brontë received three proposals during her life, but finally married her father's curate, Arthur Bell Nicholls, in 1854. She died during pregnancy a few months later, in March 1855.

QUEST FOR LOVE

A further, obvious, theme is Jane's quest for love. Before the novel has even begun Jane has lost the love of her natural parents, as well as that of her uncle, through their respective deaths. Belatedly, she finds a degree of maternal love in Bessie, but quickly loses it again as she is taken to school at Lowood. She has never experienced any kind of affection from her cousins, but seems to find a sisterly love in Helen Burns, who then dies. Again, she finds a motherly love in Miss Temple, but she loses this when her mentor leaves. Jane therefore decides to move on and once more seems to find a kind of motherly love in Mrs Fairfax, and herself becomes a mother-figure for little Adèle. Mr Rochester, in the meantime, seems to become a dangerous father-figure who then betrays her. She therefore flees Thornfield and finally discovers a lasting sisterly love with Diana and Mary. She at first finds a brotherly love in St John, but soon loses this when he proposes to her.

Eventually, of course, Jane finds a passionate and companionable love with Rochester, now reduced to her level through his injuries, blindness and loss of property. One message here seems to be that life and love are basically cruel and that happiness can only truly be achieved at a price. However, Charlotte Brontë also seems to attack the Victorian convention of brotherly and sisterly love as the basis for marriage, in favour of the new ideal of companionship, based on equality.

RELIGIOUS FAITH

The novel also, at its core, deals with religious faith – hence the uproar amongst **Evangelicals** when it was published. It addresses the meaning of religion and its relevance to the individual's behaviour. Jane sees different forms of religious practice at Lowood, encounters Rochester who wants to reform morality for his own convenience at Thornfield and is finally subject to St John Rivers's ideas of religious self-sacrifice at Moor House. Every character who professes some kind of religious faith is subject to some form of **ironic** commentary. Charlotte Brontë suggests that behaviour driven by what society thinks is proper can all too easily be confused with behaviour motivated by religious beliefs. And the novel asks if morality can simply be remade as a social convention, or whether it is something more.

KEY QUOTATION: RELIGIOUS FAITH **A01**

During his examination of Jane, at Gateshead, Brocklehurst asks her '"Do you read your Bible?" "Sometimes." "With pleasure? Are you fond of it?" "I like Revelations, and the Book of Daniel, and Genesis, and Samuel, and a little bit of Exodus, and some parts of Kings and Chronicles, and Job and Jonah." "And the Psalms? I hope you like them?" "No, sir." "No? Oh, shocking!"' (Chapter 4, p. 40)

Possible interpretations:

- Jane's choice of the particular Old and New Testament books cited implies that she is passionate and drawn, at this stage in her life, to dramatic **narrative**. But – as Brocklehurst's reply indicates – Jane's responses and her tastes are unconventional. At this time a child was expected to like the Bible, and simply memorise the Psalms.

- There is irony in this dialogue. Brocklehurst's observations suggest that he may not be Jane's equal in exegesis (interpretation of the Bible), though she is a child of ten and he is an educated man.

- This conversation would have told Victorian readers much about Jane's intellect and her faith, and about Brocklehurst's mediocrity and the inadequate religious and educational regime under which Jane was soon to be schooled.

PART FOUR: STRUCTURE, FORM AND LANGUAGE

STRUCTURE

COINCIDENCES?

The novel is very tightly constructed and the form is dictated by its major theme: Jane's growing up. There is a certain amount of coincidence at work, but only to the extent that coincidences also happen in fairy stories, and the author is playing with these patterns quite deliberately. Charlotte Brontë wanted to write about what is 'true', in other words what is deeply felt, genuine and sincere, as much as what is observed or 'real' and we can see this in the composition of the novel as much as in its content.

JANE'S ROLE IN THE STRUCTURE

The structure of the novel is deceptively organic and free-flowing, and lacks a traditional moral framework which marks a radical departure from the majority of novels in Charlotte Brontë's day. In effect it is given structural unity by Jane, who carries the theme of growing up while she searches for a way to build her own identity and resolve the tensions within her character. Because of this and her movements to and from Thornfield, the book falls roughly into five phases, which do not quite correspond with the three volumes of the original edition (see **Part One: *Jane Eyre* in context**). At the end of each phase Jane moves on to a new stage in her development: at Gateshead she is still a child; when she leaves for Lowood she moves into girlhood; she is an adolescent at Thornfield; she reaches maturity at Morton/Marsh End/Moor House; and she becomes fulfilled with her marriage to Rochester at Ferndean. This structure is suggestive of growth and supports the theme by showing the reader how Jane develops.

STUDY FOCUS: REPETITION AND PARALLELS A02

The use of repetition in the novel, especially in Jane's flight from Rochester and her flight from St John, provides it with an alternative to the more linear structure provided by the theme of Jane's progress towards maturity. In the thematic structure of the novel, the Jane–Rivers relationship develops in direct contrast to the Jane–Rochester relationship. This enables us to see exactly what is at stake for Jane, who must resolve the tension between passion and self-control in order to live a happy and fulfilled life. On both occasions she struggles to maintain her identity and the two characters effectively **symbolise** different aspects of her self. The parallels are made clear when she says 'I was almost as hard beset by him [St John] now as I had been once before, in a different way, by another [Rochester]' (Chapter XXXV, p. 482). What different shape would the novel have had if Jane had married St John?

FORM

NARRATIVE AND POINT OF VIEW

The **narrative** focuses entirely on Jane. Events only appear in the novel because they have an impact on her growth into an independent, moral and strong-minded woman and we are only interested in other characters' experiences because Jane can learn from them. Every character and incident therefore has some bearing on her development and, in this way, the theme of the novel is brought alive; every detail is made to count. We are never surprised by a new development of Jane's character as each phase, each element of character development is given a sound basis earlier on in the novel. Plot and character are **foreshadowed**.

Because the novel is a fictional autobiography and therefore consists of a first-person narrative we largely see events and characters from the **narrator's** point of view and this gives the story a high degree of authenticity. This also creates a very close bond between the narrator and the reader and draws the latter into a closer involvement with the story. The direct appeals to the reader always come at moments of heightened intensity or action, for example when Rochester asks Jane to forgive him after their first wedding day, 'Reader, I forgave him' (Chapter XXVII, p. 344), when Jane runs away from Rochester afterwards, 'Gentle reader, may you never feel what I then felt!' (Chapter XXVII, p. 370), and as we come to the close of the novel, 'Reader, I married him' (Chapter XXXVIII, p. 517).

WHAT FORM DOES *JANE EYRE* TAKE?

Jane's experience of growing up, the novel's major theme, makes it in part a **Bildungsroman**, a 'coming of age' story. But, her passionate nature, which leads to her rebellion against the gendered norms and social conventions of the period, are reflected in the **Gothic** and supernatural aspects of the novel. The form of the Gothic allows a process of **defamiliarisation** to take place, which destabilises ordinary everyday life and therefore puts the reader in a position where they are able to question what is normally taken for granted.

The novel also takes the form of a romance, though by dwelling sympathetically on the prospective death of one of Jane's suitors in the closing lines, the ending is not as conventional as her marriage to Rochester might at first make it seem. And, there are also aspects of a quest narrative too, which go some way to explaining the fairy-tale coincidences, though the quest is not conventionally achieved. The novel therefore uses, but also adapts, established forms, so that in the end it is not quite an autobiography, nor a Gothic novel, nor a **Romantic** quest narrative, nor a romance, nor a fairy tale – though in a way it is all of these.

> **CRITICAL VIEWPOINT** **A03**
>
> Fairy tales very commonly use repetitive structures and established patterns, in part because they were once passed on purely orally and repetition enabled the teller to remember the tale. Charlotte Brontë seems to make her own use of repetition, which creates the effect of a fairy tale and reinforces her use of fairy-tale **imagery** and language.

REVISION FOCUS: TASK 4 **A02**

Consider the following:

● The importance of dreams and the supernatural for prefiguring events in *Jane Eyre*.

● The importance of fairy tales in *Jane Eyre*.

Write opening paragraphs for essays based on these discussion points. Set out your arguments clearly and ensure that your paragraphs link to each other in a logical way.

LANGUAGE

NAMES

Charlotte Brontë wrote very carefully, drafting out every passage before writing it up and she spent a considerable amount of time on small details such as the choice of names. 'Eyre', for instance, came from a family called Eyre whose historic house had a room in it which reportedly housed a 'madwoman', but Charlotte Brontë also used the name because it carried with it the sense of being as free as air, a faint reference to the sprite Ariel and the suggestion of an eagle's eyrie. Where the name 'Reed' suggests a certain pliability, 'Rivers' suggests the pull of strong currents and the influence of forces beyond the individual's control. 'Temple' suggests a place of worship, safety and goodness. 'Jane' hints at 'plain Jane'.

COLLOQUIALISM

Charlotte Brontë frequently uses **colloquialisms** such as 'on hands' (p. 478) in *Jane Eyre*. This might be read as reflecting her own upbringing and use of language, as local **dialect** was much more commonplace and more widely accepted in the first half of the nineteenth century than it is today. However, it may also be the author's intention to create a sense of realism in the language used by her characters.

SIMPLICITY OF LANGUAGE

The descriptive passages of the novel draw us into the action, and though their style is often quite **journalistic** – 'It was the fifteenth of January, about nine o'clock in the morning Bessie was gone down to breakfast; my cousins had not yet been summoned to their mamma' (Chapter IV, p. 36) – they are highly suggestive: 'Terrible moment: full of struggle, blackness, burning! Not a human being that ever lived could wish to be loved better than I was loved; and him who thus loved me I absolutely worshipped: and I must renounce love and idol' (Chapter XXVII, p. 363).

The dialogue in the novel is especially important because it reflects the education, station and attitude of the characters; with respect to Adèle it is also indicative of her nationality and training. The extensive use of French in the novel adds veracity to Adèle's exchanges with Jane and makes Jane's own accomplishments more tangible. The dialogue also allows us an insight into the minds of the characters, brings them alive and is generally much more convincing than anything written by Charlotte Brontë's predecessors.

CHECK THE BOOK A01

Both *Jane Eyre* and Emily Brontë's *Wuthering Heights* make use of dialect. The first readers of *Wuthering Heights* found its language too coarse, and Charlotte edited it to remove some of the dialect (this edition is no longer popular). Although Charlotte uses dialect in *Jane Eyre*, she does so perhaps more carefully and more sparingly than her sister.

CONTEXT A04

Jane's use of the word 'idol' draws our attention to the Bible's Ten Commandments. As an Anglican, Charlotte Brontë would have been familiar with two commandments referring to false worship. Here, Jane is referring to the Second Commandment: 'Thou shalt not make unto thee any graven image' (from the Holy Bible, King James version, Exodus 20:3–18).

CONTEXT A04

The use of French and references to other languages are indicative of the level of education Charlotte Brontë and her readers possessed.

CONVERSATION

The conversations between Jane and Rochester feel entirely natural and give us a real sense of their love for each other. Jane and Rochester express themselves very directly, and everything from their banter to their most impassioned exchanges is suggestive of deeply felt and genuine affection.

It is also interesting to see how Jane automatically corrects Hannah's English when she first talks to the servant as her superior in Chapter XXIX:

'I am no beggar; any more than yourself or your young ladies.'
After a pause, she said, 'I dunnut understand that: you've like no house, nor no brass, I guess?'
'The want of house or brass (by which I suppose you mean money) does not make a beggar in your sense of the word.' (p. 391–2)

This suggests that Jane is acutely sensitive of her social position at this point, and hints at the snobbery of her childhood when she could not 'purchase liberty at the price of caste' (Chapter III, p. 30) (see **Empire** in **Part Five: Contexts and critical debates**).

> **CONTEXT** **A04**
>
> Despite her rebellious nature, Jane still reflects many of the dominant attitudes of her class and time. Charlotte Brontë could also be a snob; she looked down, for instance, on one of her father's curates – who proposed to her – because he came from Dublin and was therefore not, in her view, her social equal.

STUDY FOCUS: A MIND IN TORMENT **A01**

Charlotte Brontë's language is at its most powerful when she is describing a mind in torment. The heart of the novel therefore lies in Jane's descriptions of what is going on in her own mind. Her feelings, especially 'Conscience' and 'Passion' (Chapter XXVII, p. 343), are often given their own voice and they frequently act out a kind of drama or inner **morality play** within Jane, in which they fight over the right to determine her actions. Chapter XXVII, in which Jane determines to leave Rochester, provides us with an excellent example of this. These moments of **personification** make us aware of Jane's deepest feelings and we need to consider the degree to which they help us to understand why she acts as she does.

IMAGERY AND SYMBOLISM

THE USE OF IMAGERY IN *JANE EYRE*

Imagery and **symbolism** help unite the novel and are as important to the **narrative** as the action and plot. The novel is full of uncanny, faintly **Gothic**, references to local **folklore**, fairy tales, ghosts and sprites. Jane is driven back to Rochester when she mysteriously hears his voice calling to her when St John Rivers presses her to marry him. But the core of the novel actually lies in Jane's descriptions of what goes on in her mind and it is in these descriptions that we find the most striking use of imagery.

Charlotte Brontë sources her imagery from literature, especially from Shakespeare and the **Romantics**, the Bible, and, for the large supernatural element in the novel, from her own upbringing. Some of the images are quite commonplace, but nonetheless when repeated help form clear links between the various characters. Rochester often likens Jane to an eager little bird, for example, meaning she is physically small and mentally agile, but Jane also likens herself to the 'stray and stranger birds' (Chapter XXII, p. 282) that Rochester

throws his crumbs to. After Jane has run away from Rochester, her heart becomes 'impotent as a bird' which, 'with both wings broken … still quivered its shattered pinions in vain attempts to seek him' (Chapter XXVIII, p. 373). And when the Rivers offer her a home, St John likens her to 'a half frozen bird [which] some wintry wind might have driven through their casement' (Chapter XXIX, p. 400). When she returns to Rochester she finds that he is like a 'fettered wild beast or bird' (Chapter XXXVII, p. 497) and that, as they enter the final stage of their relationship in which he has to depend on her, he has become 'a royal eagle, chained to a perch' which is 'forced to entreat a sparrow to become its purveyor' (Chapter XXXVII, p. 507).

REFLECTIONS

An imaginative link, which draws more directly on Charlotte Brontë's knowledge of folklore, is formed between Jane and Bertha. When Jane sees herself in the mirror of the red-room she sees herself as a ghost, as utterly alien and other, and she is referred to as a sprite and a witch by Rochester. These may be read as quite playful references to the supernatural, but they take on a new import when Bertha is described as a vampire. This feeds into the Gothic tone of the Thornfield section of the text and shows us how Jane herself might fall victim to her passions and become another Bertha. It also shows us how isolated Jane is from her family and her society.

THE CHESTNUT TREE

It is interesting to see how Thornfield Hall is often symbolically identified with its master, in appearance, and when it is destroyed. For instance, Thornfield Hall is dour and quiet when Jane first arrives, just as its master is, then gradually regains light and life. One of the most powerful images in the novel is that of the shattered chestnut tree that stands in its grounds. This tree initially has the role of an omen. As a symbol of life it is quite fitting that Rochester proposes to Jane under its boughs. However, split in two by a violent storm that very night it forewarns us of the disaster to come: the failed wedding day and Mr Rochester's injury, and as such fills Jane's thoughts with foreboding before their wedding. It finally reappears at the end of the novel when Rochester proposes for the second time: 'I am no better than the old lightning-struck chestnut-tree in Thornfield orchard' (Chapter XXXVII, p. 512). In other words the tree, initially a simple object in the novel, is transformed by events into a complex image and powerful symbol of Jane and Rochester's relationship.

IMAGERY FROM BOOKS

A key feature of the novel is the symbolic use of literature. We learn a lot about the characters and their situation from what they read. The novel opens on a depressing November afternoon which reflects the mood of Jane Eyre herself who is trying to escape by reading Bewick's *History of British Birds*. This book is full of images of shipwrecks, storms, Arctic wastes, high mountain reaches, death and disaster and it seems to reflect Jane's own feelings about life at Gateshead. She also reads *Gulliver's Travels* as a kind of escape and the *Arabian Nights* where she learns about magic. Helen Burns, however, prefers *Rasselas*, a dry tome about the placid endurance of life and reality. Whereas Jane prefers to read texts that feed into her passions, Helen hopes to learn about the real world and the necessity of self-control.

CONTEXT **A04**

The storm is a reminder that shipwrecks were frequently used to signal disaster in Victorian novels.

HISTORICAL BACKGROUND

THE POSITION OF WOMEN

CHECK THE BOOK **A04**

For more detail on the cultural background to the novel see R. Gilmour, *The Victorian Period: The Intellectual and Cultural Context of English Literature* 1830–1890 (1993).

CHECK THE BOOK **A03**

In *Villette* (1853) Charlotte Brontë revisited the theme of an isolated but respectable young woman needing to seek work as a teacher. In this case, much of the novel was set in Belgium, and based on experiences in Brontë's own life. It is a much more despairing novel, and the protagonist, Lucy Snowe, though she shares much with Jane Eyre, is more enigmatic.

Jane Eyre is a strong female **protagonist**, created by Charlotte Brontë at a time when women's talents, skills and independence were far from being valued. Brontë was well aware of the subservient position of women in Victorian society and of the difficulties that were faced by women who wanted or had to make their own way in the world. At this point it was not respectable for a middle-class woman to earn her own living; she was expected to make a career out of marriage or at least to confine her public interests to doing unpaid charitable work. If a young middle-class woman had to support herself and wanted to maintain her class position and reputation, she really only had one option: to work as a governess. The governess was therefore in an anomalous social position because she was neither a servant, due to her class, nor a proper young lady.

Charlotte Brontë was especially sensitive to the difficulties faced by these young women because she herself had worked as a teacher and as a governess, and hoped to make a career out of writing. This lends a special poignancy to Jane's story as in many respects it was based on Charlotte Brontë's own and her sister's experience. Charlotte Brontë also read widely on the subject of the position of women thanks to the large number of articles and books that were being published on this issue in the 1840s. It is not useful to overemphasise the significance of the author's biography here – Charlotte Brontë herself said that

though Jane Eyre looked like her, they had nothing else in common – but the theme of the novel was deeply felt by its author and this should be borne in mind.

SOCIAL UNREST

Other than her consideration of the position of women, Charlotte Brontë draws relatively sketchily on the history of the time at which the novel is set – around the turn of the eighteenth to nineteenth centuries. This was a period of considerable social unrest; there was widespread concern that the British labourer would go the way of the French in the Revolution of 1789. When Jane comments adversely on her pupil's French disposition, she is therefore expressing the sceptical views of her time, this being the period of the French wars with Britain (ending with the Battle of Waterloo in 1815). In a similar vein, there are also various allusions to the French Revolution. In Chapter XXXIII, for example, 'Famous equality and fraternisation' (p. 447) speaks obliquely of the slogan 'Liberty, Equality, Fraternity'. Beyond this, there are very few historical references.

EMPIRE

The novel does however draw extensively on the imperial context. For instance, the slave trade had only been abolished in 1807 in British territories, after a long-fought campaign by a number of organisations including the Quakers, while emancipation (the abolition of slavery itself) was only achieved in 1833. During the period 1781–1807 Britain had carried in excess of a million slaves from Africa to the Americas. As a 'Creole' (Chapter XXVI, p. 337) (see **Glossary** in **Part Two: Chapter XXVI**), Bertha Mason would probably have counted slaves traded by France – which initially abolished slavery during the Revolution – among her ancestors. Beyond this we have references to trade with the Caribbean and missionary activity in India, including Jane's comment that '**I was not heroic enough to purchase liberty at the price of caste**' (Chapter III, p. 30) – all part of the economic, political and social context in which Charlotte Brontë was writing.

CONTEXT **A04**

Jane refers to 'caste' (Chapter III, p. 30) in reflecting on her future. Caste was an Indian concept that drew on a hierarchy that was religious, as well as social and economic, and one that was designated by birth rather than experience.

LITERARY BACKGROUND

CHARLOTTE BRONTË'S READING

CHECK THE BOOK **A04**

For more on the general prose context of the period see H. Fraser with D. Brown, *English Prose of the Nineteenth Century* (1996).

Charlotte Brontë read widely as a child and as a young woman while she lived at home in her father's rectory in Haworth. She and her brother and sisters were encouraged to dip into Aesop, the Bible, Homer, Virgil, Shakespeare, Milton, Thomson, Goldsmith, Pope, Byron, Scott, Southey, Wordsworth, *The Arabian Nights' Entertainments*, plus critical and political articles published in periodicals such as *Blackwood's Magazine*, *Fraser's Magazine* and *The Edinburgh Review*. They also read from illustrated annuals such as *The Gem*, *The Amulet* and *Friendship's Offering*.

Charlotte Brontë may have lost the strong religious sensibility of her earlier years by the time that she wrote *Jane Eyre*, but her early literary training continued to be influential in all her novels. The **sagas**, poetry and dramas that the Brontë children wrote provide ample evidence of the influence of this diverse reading and are full of **melodrama**, passion, the weird and wonderful, and keenly felt moral themes. This helps explain why *Jane Eyre* seems to be a mixture of the **Gothic**, **Realist** and **Romantic**.

It is difficult to know exactly who Charlotte Brontë read in later life, but we know from the dedication which appears in the second edition of *Jane Eyre* that she read Thackeray who, like Trollope, George Eliot and Dickens, shared her dislike of **Evangelicalism**. Mrs Gaskell was her friend and later her biographer.

CHARLOTTE BRONTË AND JANE AUSTEN

There do, however, appear to be some interesting gaps in Charlotte Brontë's literary history. For instance, at the time that *Jane Eyre* was being written (published in 1847), Jane Austen was already a well-established author (*Pride and Prejudice* was published in 1813), but it does not appear that Charlotte had read her. The critic G. H. Lewes in fact advised Charlotte to read some of Austen's work in order to improve her own writing. When Charlotte finished reading *Pride and Prejudice*, however, she wrote to Lewes explaining that Austen was altogether useless to her and was not even, really, a novelist. In her letters to him in 1848 she argued that Jane Austen was 'without poetry' and 'cannot be great' (18 January), allowing that she was 'only shrewd and observant' (12 January) and 'sensible (more real than true)' (18 January).

MODERN TEXTS

Jane Eyre has been an influential text and not all criticism comes in the form of non-fiction prose. The novel has been replied to in the form of prequel, Rhys's *Wide Sargasso Sea* and rewritten, for example, by Angela Carter, who explores the theme of Bluebeard in *The Magic Toyshop*. It has also influenced popular modern romantic **narratives** such as Daphne du Maurier's *Rebecca* (1938).

STUDY FOCUS: *WIDE SARGASSO SEA* · A03

Jean Rhys's *Wide Sargasso Sea* (1966) tells the story of Rochester's life in the Caribbean from the first Mrs Rochester's point of view, rather than Jane's, and provides the reader with a very different understanding of the original narrative. More recently, critics such as Peter Hulme have stressed that though it remains important to take a critical view of *Jane Eyre* in light of Jean Rhys's novel, Jean Rhys herself can be categorised as a member of the 'white colonial elite', while her novel is 'sympathetic to the planter class ruined by emancipation' (*Colonial Discourse/Postcolonial Theory* (1994), p. 72). *Wide Sargasso Sea* remains an excellent companion text for *Jane Eyre* in a comparative study.

CHECK THE FILM · A04

Jean Rhys's *Wide Sargasso Sea* was made into an atmospheric and highly charged film by John Duigan in 1993.

CRITICAL DEBATES

RECEPTION AND EARLY CRITICAL REVIEWS

Jane Eyre was well received and a bestseller when it was first published. But there was also widespread censure of the novel on social and moral grounds due to its critical representation of religious sentiment, its easy acceptance of a love which transcends class and, finally, its author's vivid portrayal of emotion. Elizabeth Rigby, for instance, writing for a conservative periodical in 1848, felt that 'the tone of mind and thought which has overthrown authority and violated every code human and divine ,,, is the same which has also written *Jane Eyre*' (Elizabeth Rigby, 'A review of *Vanity Fair* and *Jane Eyre*', *Quarterly Review*, No. CLXVII, December, 1848, pp. 82–99).

CHECK THE BOOK **A04**

For a discussion of the ways in which Charlotte Brontë's reputation, that of *Jane Eyre* and that of Jane have been intertwined, see Lucasta Miller, *The Brontë Myth* (2002).

Thus, in the 1840s, *Jane Eyre* was a revolutionary text. Victorian critics did not like Jane Eyre's strong-minded independence and many thought that the novel was coarse. The novel was blamed for the corruption of contemporary tastes and morality, in both life and art. Most contemporary critics felt that there was something dangerous in the novel's underlying message, while Jane Eyre herself was seen as godless and unrestrained. Others thought that Charlotte Brontë's personality was reflected in the novel and that that personality was irredeemably vulgar and alien. Such a view was only changed after Mrs Gaskell's biography of Charlotte Brontë was published, and Charlotte Brontë herself worked hard at rescuing the reputation of the book.

EARLY TWENTIETH-CENTURY VIEWS

Up until the 1970s twentieth-century critics like Lord David Cecil in *Early Victorian Novelists* (1934) were scathing in their assessment of *Jane Eyre* because of the way in which the novel operates, in part, as a fairy tale or as a simple **narrative** of wish fulfilment. This, in their view, put the novel beyond the bounds of a serious adult readership while, at the same time, they accused it of being a baggy, rather artless blend of undisciplined daydreams. Charlotte Brontë was supposed to have written incoherently, without form, restraint, observation or analysis. The narrative was said to be held up by unnecessary passages of over-poetic prose. The plot was accused of moving forward thanks to a combination of good luck and coincidence, while the novel itself was assumed to lack composition. However, others, such as Q. D. Leavis in her introduction to the Penguin edition of *Jane Eyre* in 1966, defended the novel and argued that it was in fact very tightly composed, and that its structure was coherent and thoroughly controlled in the interest of the theme. She argued that Jane Eyre's thoughts and feelings are not simply observed but, more importantly, imagined on the deepest level.

Marxist criticism

During the 1970s new readings of the novel began to emerge, most notably those of Marxists and feminists. Marxist critics, like Raymond Williams in *The English Novel from Dickens to Lawrence* (1970) and Terry Eagleton in *Myths of Power: A Marxist study of the Brontës* (1975), reassessed the context in which the Brontë sisters' books were written and read. They were especially interested in the ambiguity of Jane's employment as governess and her social mobility, which reveal the social contradictions and tensions of Charlotte Brontë's

own time. Williams stressed that the period in which the Brontë sisters were writing was one of unprecedented social change. The tensions of this period, he argued, are reflected both in the representation of Jane's passion and desire (for a man above her station), and in the fear of isolation that we see more generally in *Jane Eyre*. The novel's passion is then communicated through a kind of private conversation between **narrator** and reader and this, in his view, is what makes it new.

Eagleton, in turn, argued that the central problem or key theme in *Jane Eyre* is submission and the point at which this ceases to be a

good thing. Charlotte Brontë, in Eagleton's view, sought a balance between the social and moral conventions of her day and self-fulfilment. Due to this, in *Jane Eyre*, Jane negotiates her way between these opposing urges and manages to climb the social ladder, quite properly – thanks to an inheritance and good behaviour – *and* on her own terms.

Feminist criticism

Feminist critics in the 1970s read *Jane Eyre* as a radical text in which a woman writer wrote successfully about the treatment of women in her society. In this way, feminists, such as Sandra Gilbert and Susan Gubar in *The Madwoman in the Attic: The Woman Writer and the Nineteenth-Century Literary Imagination* (1979), picked up on the issues that so distressed the book's original, Victorian critics. Most commentators in fact now tend to stress the underlying political purpose of the novel in which Jane acts as a defender of women. This works because, though the plot is like that of a fairy tale, it has been transposed to the real material world of wages and work in which Cinderella's story has quite different and much more radical implications than those it had as a simple fairy story. Gilbert and Gubar therefore say that Mrs Rigby's assessment of *Jane Eyre* as radical (see **Reception and early critical reviews**) is quite correct, whether or not the author wanted to admit it at the time.

CHECK THE BOOK A03

For a feminist analysis of Jean Rhys's *Wide Sargasso Sea* and other work see M. Humm *Border Traffic Strategies of Contemporary Women Writers* (1991).

CONTEMPORARY APPROACHES

PSYCHOANALYTICAL READINGS

Psychoanalytical readings and those that focus on myth have suggested many new and interesting readings of the novel, including the idea that Rochester's first wife is Jane's double. Bertha Mason is portrayed as being mentally ill, unable to speak and physically and mentally resembling a savage wild animal. She is kept under lock and key, and is treated as a thing rather than as a human being. She therefore seems to be the opposite of Jane who is a calm English governess, rational, self-controlled, articulate and small. However, as Elizabeth Imlay has noted in *Charlotte Brontë and the Mysteries of Love: Myth and Allegory in Jane Eyre* (1989), both women are represented at different times in very similar ways.

Jane describes Bertha as a ghost or a vampire after the wedding veil is torn. This is a frightening **image**, but Mr Rochester similarly thinks of Jane as an imp, spirit and witch. Bertha is presented as 'mad', and Jane is said to behave like 'a mad cat' (p. 15). Bertha scratches and bites, and Jane scratches her cousin John Reed. Bertha is tied to a chair and locked in a room, Jane is told to sit in a chair and is locked in the red-room. In other words, when Jane follows her passions and loses her self-control, she behaves and is punished like Bertha. When she is frustrated by her life at Thornfield Jane goes up onto the third floor to daydream, at which point she is physically and mentally close to Bertha. In this way we become aware of the thin dividing line between Jane and Bertha if Jane followed her basest instincts. Bertha's death therefore **symbolises** the sacrifice of the most passionate part of Jane's self.

POSTCOLONIAL CRITICISM

Postcolonial criticism aims to expose the unequal power relationships that exist between the West and the East (the colonies) and to do so by giving the colonial subject – that is, someone who is subject to imperial power – a voice of their own, on their own terms. Gayatri Spivak in *Critical Inquiry* 12 (1) 1985, therefore criticised the kind of psychological approach outline above, and argued that Jane Eyre's rise as an independent woman is dependent upon the fall and dehumanisation of a colonial subject. As such, it is argued that the novel reflects the patterns of imperialism. Edward Said in *Orientalism* (1978) had by this point highlighted the importance of colonialism and images of imperialism and empire in

Jane Eyre. Jane is clearly a white middle-class Protestant who believes in healthy good deeds and hard work. When she runs away from Thornfield she says that she will try to turn her hand to anything that is honest. However, she still draws the line at travelling to India where, she fears, she would collapse and die, as St John eventually does. This rational approach to life apparently allows her to have the self-control that Bertha Mason lacks, which in Victorian eyes was quite natural.

CHECK THE FILM A03

The best twentieth-century film and stage versions of the novel, those like Franco Zeffireli's 1996 version that capture its underlying emotion and sexual tension, were influenced by contemporary, post-Freudian, interpretations of the novel. But it is important to go back to the book as adaptations will say more about the time at which they are made than they will about the original text.

STUDY FOCUS: BERTHA MASON **A04**

Bertha Mason's story is itself a colonial **narrative**. Rochester marries her purely for her property. In fact, he went to the Caribbean just to seek his fortune and, like other English adventurers, found unbridled passion as well as a solution to his financial difficulties. Interestingly, the sexual partners that Rochester tells Jane about (p. 359) are all foreign, which was not unusual at this time. In the Victorian era, foreign women were often thought to be more highly sexed than English women, but, more importantly, the very fact that they were different and 'exotic' also made them particularly attractive to some English men. Foreign shores and people were seen as dangerous, essentially unhealthy, wild, yet alluring in the British novels of the period, and Charlotte Brontë has made full use of this widespread colonial imagery. Bertha is treated and seen as a thing rather than a human being because she is a Creole (see **Glossary** in **Part Two: Chapter XXVI**), not just because she is unstable. And, as suggested by Rochester's desperate need to leave the West Indies, it is suggested that only Britain can provide a safe haven for the English.

> **CHECK THE BOOK A03**
>
> For a general study of postcolonial writing (a genre and period to which Jean Rhys's work belongs) see B. Ashcroft, G. Griffiths and H. Tiffin *The Empire Writes Back: Theory and Practice in Post-Colonial Literatures* (2002).

DISABILITY CRITICISM

The most recent criticism falls within the emergent field of disability studies. For example, David Bolt, Julia Miele Rodas and Elizabeth J. Donaldson's *The Madwoman and the Blindman: Jane Eyre, Discourse, Disability* (2012) contains essays addressing all of the major and some of the minor characters, and issues of care, illness, and physical and sensory impairment within the novel. It takes *Jane Eyre* as its focus and argues that it is not possible to read the novel 'without a serious consideration of disability' (p. xii). The other forms of criticism, they observe, are still entirely valid, but 'they are all largely ignorant of the basic facts about disability' (p. x). This approach takes disability seriously on its own terms, not as a **metaphor**. So, for example, it is observed that though Rochester regains his sight to some degree, Jane marries him before this happens, and after the fire he remains an amputee. In this way the novel does not conform to the Victorian model of the 'school of pain' in which a character suffers a temporary disability or infirmity but eventually recovers once they have changed their erring ways. Also, as Martha Stoddard Holmes argues, whereas Victorian novelists usually brush over physical conditions, 'Brontë's description of Rochester after the fire ... is frank and direct' (p. 161). Rochester's disability is perfectly real.

PART SIX: GRADE BOOSTER

ASSESSMENT FOCUS

WHAT ARE YOU BEING ASKED TO FOCUS ON?

The questions or tasks you are set will be based around the four **Assessment Objectives, AO1** to **AO4**.

You may get more marks for certain **AOs** than others depending on which unit you're working on. Check with your teacher if you are unsure.

WHAT DO THESE AOS ACTUALLY MEAN?

ASSESSMENT OBJECTIVES		MEANING?
AO1	Articulate creative, informed and relevant responses to literary texts, using appropriate terminology and concepts, and coherent, accurate written expression.	You write about texts in accurate, clear and precise ways so that what you have to say is clear to the marker. You use literary terms (e.g. **Bildungsroman**) or refer to concepts (e.g. **personification**) in relevant places.
AO2	Demonstrate detailed critical understanding in analysing the ways in which structure, form and language shape meanings in literary texts.	You show that you understand the specific techniques and methods used by the writer(s) to create the text (e.g. **foreshadowing**, **melodrama**, **pathos**, etc.). You can explain clearly how these methods affect the meaning.
AO3	Explore connections and comparisons between different literary texts, informed by interpretations of other readers.	You are able to see relevant links between different texts. You are able to comment on how others (such as critics) view the text.
AO4	Demonstrate understanding of the significance and influence of the contexts in which literary texts are written and received.	You can explain how social, historical, political or personal backgrounds to the texts affected the writer and how the texts were read when they were first published and at different times since.

WHAT DOES THIS MEAN FOR YOUR STUDY OR REVISION?

Depending on the course you are following, you could be asked to:

- Respond to a general question about the text as a whole. For example:

Explore the ways Charlotte Brontë uses the uncanny and the supernatural in *Jane Eyre*.

- Write about an aspect of *Jane Eyre* which is also a feature of other texts you are studying. These questions may take the form of a challenging statement or quotation which you are invited to discuss. For example:

To what extent do you agree that Gothic literature's prime concern is the effect of defamiliarisation?

- Focus on the particular similarities, links, contrasts and differences between this text and others. For example:

Compare the ways writers use fairy tales in *Jane Eyre* and the other text(s) you are studying.

EXAMINER'S TIP ✓

Make sure you know how many marks are available for each AO in the task you are set. This can help you divide up your time or decide how much attention to give each aspect.

TARGETING A HIGH GRADE

It is very important to understand the progression from a lower grade to a high grade. In all cases, it is not enough simply to mention some key points and references – instead, you should explore them in depth, drawing out what is interesting and relevant to the question or issue.

TYPICAL C GRADE FEATURES

FEATURES	EXAMPLES
AO1 You use critical vocabulary accurately, and your arguments make sense, are relevant and focus on the task. You show detailed knowledge of the text.	*The descriptive passages in the opening chapter, especially phrases such as 'drear November day' (Chapter I, p. 10) are typical of Charlotte Brontë's use of pathos.*
AO2 You can say how some specific aspects of form, structure and language shape meanings.	*The use of visual contrasts, such as those between the two clergymen Brocklehurst and Rivers, provides a point of comparison as to the similarities and differences in their characters.*
AO3 You consider in detail the connections between texts, and also how interpretations of texts differ with some relevant supporting references.	*Antoinette's story, depicted in "Wide Sargasso Sea", gives the reader access to Bertha Mason/Rochester's point of view, and enables us to empathise with the torment that she undergoes.* *In both "The Magic Toyshop" and "Jane Eyre", the tantalising and passionately desired possibility of escape into a better life is revealed to be much more difficult than it at first seems to be.*
AO4 You can write about a range of contextual factors and make some specific and detailed links between these and the task or text.	*The negative portrayal of Evangelicalism in the novel is probably a reflection of Charlotte Brontë's upbringing; as a clergyman's daughter she was almost certainly well aware of contemporary religious debate.*

TYPICAL FEATURES OF AN A OR A* RESPONSE

FEATURES	EXAMPLES
AO1 You use appropriate critical vocabulary and a technically fluent style. Your arguments are well structured, coherent and always relevant with a very sharp focus on task.	*Jane's choice of book provides us with an insight into her current position and state of mind. The Arctic wastes and sublime landscapes of Berwick's "History of British Birds" reinforce the setting and reflect the bitterness of Jane's isolation; its shipwrecks foreshadow the crises yet to come.*
AO2 You explore and analyse key aspects of form, structure and language and evaluate perceptively how they shape meanings.	*Red, the colour of fire and passion, is always present in the pivotal moments of Jane's journey to maturity, such as that which occurs in the 'red-room'. But, Jane must learn to control her passions; otherwise she will be fatally consumed by them like Bertha Rochester.*
AO3 You show a detailed and perceptive understanding of issues raised through connections between texts and can consider different interpretations with a sharp evaluation of their strengths and weaknesses. You have a range of excellent supportive references.	*Although Rochester says in "Jane Eyre" that he has 'done all that God and humanity' might have asked, it appears from Part Two of "Wide Sargasso Sea" that all he wanted from Antoinette/Bertha was 'to break her up', which he did. And, though, in "Wide Sargasso Sea" we seem to gain access to Bertha Mason's point of view, Rhys's deliberate use of ambiguity and play with language leaves us uncertain about her own interpretation of her experiences. What we therefore gain a sense of is Rochester's cruelty and that Bertha/ Antoinette's path to destruction is inescapable.*
AO4 You show deep, detailed and relevant understanding of how contextual factors link to the text or task.	*The critique of Evangelicalism that is an inherent part of the depiction of Brocklehurst's hypocrisy – and which was commented on adversely as irreligious by some of the original readers of the novel – was likely to have been a reflection of Charlotte Brontë's upbringing. As a clergyman's daughter she would have been well aware of religious debate at the time that she was writing, and at that point Evangelicalism sought reforms of the Anglican Church that were not always welcomed by its established ministers.*

HOW TO WRITE HIGH-QUALITY RESPONSES

The quality of your writing – how you express your ideas – is vital for getting a higher grade, and **AO1** and **AO2** are specifically about **how** you respond.

FIVE KEY AREAS

The quality of your responses can be broken down into **five** key areas.

1. THE STRUCTURE OF YOUR ANSWER/ESSAY

- First, get **straight to the point in your opening paragraph**. Use a sharp, direct first sentence that deals with a key aspect and then follow up with evidence or detailed reference.
- **Put forward an argument or point of view** (you won't **always** be able to challenge or take issue with the essay question, but generally, where you can, you are more likely to write in an interesting way).
- **Signpost your ideas** with connectives and references, which help the essay flow.
- **Don't repeat points already made**, not even in the conclusion, unless you have something new to say that adds a further dimension.

TARGETING A HIGH GRADE **AO1**

Here's an example of an opening paragraph that gets straight to the point, addressing the question: **'Learning how to control her passions is necessary for Jane to achieve happiness.' How do you respond to this viewpoint?**

'Then you will not yield?' Rochester asks Jane, 'No' she replies. In choosing to leave Thornfield and that which she 'wholly' loves it appears that Jane has finally learned how to control her passions. With nothing to her name but her reputation, she engages successfully in a 'frantic effort of principle'. But, she is not able to achieve happiness until she returns to her employer, and that requires not only a change in both of their circumstances, but also that she learns to acknowledge her desires.

Immediate focus on task and key words and example from text

2. USE OF TITLES, NAMES, ETC.

This is a simple, but important, tip to stay on the right side of the examiners.

- Make sure that you spell correctly the titles of the texts, chapters, name of authors and so on. Present them correctly, too, with double quotation marks and capitals as appropriate. For example, *'In Chapter I of "Jane Eyre" ...'*.
- Use the **full title**, unless there is a good reason not to (e.g. it's very long).
- Use the terms 'novel' or 'text' rather than ' book' or 'story'. If you use the word 'story', the examiner may think you mean the plot/action rather than the 'text' as a whole.

3. EFFECTIVE QUOTATIONS

Do not 'bolt on' quotations to the points you make. You will get some marks for including them, but examiners will not find your writing very fluent.

> **EXAMINER'S TIP** ✓
>
> Answer the question set, not the question you'd like to have been asked. Examiners say that often students will be set a question on one character (for example, Rochester) but end up writing almost as much about another (such as Jane herself). Or, they write about one aspect from the question (for example, 'lunacy') but ignore another (such as 'reason'). **Stick to the question**, and **answer all parts of it**.

The best quotations are:

- Relevant
- Not too long
- Integrated into your argument/sentence.

TARGETING A HIGH GRADE A01

Here is an example of a quotation successfully embedded in a sentence:

An indication of the Gothic tone that permeates the novel can be seen when Jane hears 'a savage, a sharp' cry in the night coming from 'just above my chamber-ceiling'.

Remember – quotations can be a well-selected set of three or four single words or phrases embedded into a sentence to build a picture or explanation, or they can be longer ones that are explored and picked apart.

4. TECHNIQUES AND TERMINOLOGY

By all means mention literary terms, techniques, conventions or people (for example, '**pathos**' or '**Romantic**' or 'Martineau') but make sure that you:

- Understand what they mean
- Are able to link them to what you're saying
- Spell them correctly.

5. GENERAL WRITING SKILLS

Try to write in a way that sounds professional and uses standard English. This does not mean that your writing will lack personality – just that it will be authoritative.

- Avoid **colloquial** or everyday expressions such as 'got', 'alright', 'OK' and so on.
- Use terms such as 'convey', 'suggest', 'imply', 'infer' to explain the writer's methods.
- Refer to 'we' when discussing the audience/reader.
- Avoid assertions and generalisations; don't just state a general point of view ('*Rochester is a Byronic hero*'), but analyse closely, with clear evidence and textual detail.

TARGETING A HIGH GRADE A01

Note the professional approach in this example:

Charlotte Brontë's depiction of Jane Eyre is far more complex and subtle than most representations of middling young women during the Victorian period. Brontë's aim is to capture and express the essence of what is normally hidden, and to enable the reader to understand 'what I then felt!' This, however, is only made clear to the 'Gentle reader', whereas those around Jane are often puzzled by her passionate outbursts and morbid-seeming withdrawals. Her family and friends stand at a distance, but we come to know, and therefore to trust, her absolutely.

GRADE BOOSTER A02

It is important to remember that *Jane Eyre* is a text created by Charlotte Brontë – thinking about the choices she makes, e.g. her choice of language and plotting, will not only alert you to her methods as an author, but also her intentions, i.e. the effect she seeks to create.

QUESTIONS WITH STATEMENTS, QUOTATIONS OR VIEWPOINTS

One type of question you may come across includes a statement, quotation or viewpoint from another reader.

These questions ask you to respond to, or argue for/against, a specific point of view or critical interpretation.

For *Jane Eyre* these questions will typically be like this:

- **Discuss the view that the novel appears to consist of a series of highly unlikely coincidences.**
- **How far do you agree with the idea that Jane's is a love story?**
- **To what extent do you agree that Jane's greatest failing is her snobbery?**
- **Discuss the view that Gothic literature is concerned with making the familiar unfamiliar.**

The key thing to remember is that you are being asked to **respond to a critical interpretation** of the text – in other words, to come up with **your own 'take'** on the idea or viewpoint in the task.

KEY SKILLS REQUIRED

The table below provides help and advice on answering this type of question.

SKILL	MEANS?	HOW DO I ACHIEVE THIS?
Consider different interpretations	There will be more than one way of looking at the given question. For example, critics might be divided about the extent to which the novel achieves its success through coincidence.	• Show you have considered these different interpretations in your answer. For example: *It is true that earlier critics saw Charlotte Brontë as stretching coincidence to breaking point. However, she always sought to reflect what is essentially 'true', what is sincere and deeply felt, and this is reflected in the novel's tightly controlled composition around a single theme.*
Write with a clear, personal voice	Your own 'take' on the question is made obvious to the marker. You are not just repeating other people's ideas, but offering what **you** think.	• Although you may mention different perspectives on the task, you should settle on your own view. • Use language that shows careful, but confident, consideration. For example: *Although it has been said that … I feel that …*
Construct a coherent argument	The examiner or marker can follow your train of thought so that your own viewpoint is clear to him or her.	• Write in clear paragraphs that deal logically with different aspects of the question. • Support what you say with well-selected and relevant evidence. • Use a range of connectives to help 'signpost' your argument. For example: *Because Charlotte Brontë sought to write about what was unconsciously hidden and unseen through the deliberate use of both fairy-tale forms and imagery – such as Rochester's description of Jane as 'half fairy, half imp' – Jane's progress appears to be full of folkloric coincidence.*

ANSWERING A 'VIEWPOINT' QUESTION

Here is an example of a typical question on *Jane Eyre*:

Discuss the view that the novel appears to consist of a series of highly unlikely coincidences.

STAGE 1: DECODE THE QUESTION

Underline/highlight the **key words**, and make sure you understand what the statement, quotation or viewpoint is saying. In this case:

- **Key words** = *Discuss/consist/series/unlikely/coincidences*
- **The viewpoint/idea expressed** = *the novel relies for its structure on a number of implausible coincidences, one after the other.*

STAGE 2: DECIDE WHAT YOUR VIEWPOINT IS

Examiners have stated that they tend to reward a strong view which is clearly put. Think about the question – can you take issue with it? Disagreeing strongly can lead to higher marks, provided you have **genuine evidence** to support your point of view. Don't disagree just for the sake of it.

STAGE 3: DECIDE HOW TO STRUCTURE YOUR ANSWER

Pick out the key points you wish to make, and decide on the order in which you will present them. Keep this basic plan to hand while you write your response.

STAGE 4: WRITE YOUR RESPONSE

You could start by expanding on the statement or viewpoint expressed in the question.

- For example, in **Paragraph 1**:

  To a modern audience, "Jane Eyre" could seem to rely too heavily on the unrealistic coming together of unexpected events. It seems implausible that Jane might just happen to stumble across her cousins, the Rivers family, when she is most in need, and the likelihood that she would later inherit and help them in turn seems to be both remote and mere wish-fulfilment.

This could help by setting up the various ideas you will choose to explore, argue for/against, and so on. But do not just repeat what the question says or just say what you are going to do. Get straight to the point. For example:

  The novel continues to have an impact, however, in part because of the power of Charlotte Brontë's characterisation and also because of the enduring relevance of her treatment of the themes of identity, free will and desire.

Then, proceed to set out the different arguments or critical perspectives, including your own. This might be done by dealing with specific aspects or elements of the novel, one by one. Consider giving 1–2 paragraphs to explore each aspect in turn. Discuss the strengths and weaknesses in each particular point of view. For example:

- **Paragraph 2:** first aspect:

  *To answer whether the critic's interpretation is valid, we need to **first of all** look at …*

  *It is clear from this that …/a **strength** of this argument is*

  *However, I believe this suggests that …/a **weakness** in this argument is*

- **Paragraph 3:** a new focus or aspect:
  Turning our attention to the critical idea that … it could be said that …

- **Paragraphs 4, 5, etc. onwards:** develop the argument, building a convincing set of points:
  Furthermore, if we look at …

- **Last paragraph:** end with a clear statement of your view, without simply listing all the points you have made:
  *To say that the novel appears to the reader to stretch coincidence too far is only partly true, as **I believe that** …*

EXAMINER'S TIP

You should comment concisely, professionally and thoughtfully and present a range of viewpoints. Try using modal verbs such as 'could', 'might', 'may' to clarify your own interpretation. For additional help on **Using critical interpretations and perspectives**, see pages 98–9.

EXAMINER'S TIP

Note how the ideas are clearly signposted through a range of connectives and linking phrases, such as 'However' and 'Turning our attention to'.

COMPARING *JANE EYRE* WITH OTHER TEXTS

As part of your assessment, you may have to compare *Jane Eyre* with, or link it to, other texts that you have studied. These may be plays, novels or even poetry. You may also have to link or draw in references from texts written by critics. For example:

> **Compare the depiction of female adolescence in *Jane Eyre* and other text(s) you have studied.**

THE TASK

Your task is likely to be on a method, issue, viewpoint or key aspect that is common to *Jane Eyre* and the other text(s), so you will need to:

> **Evaluate the issue** or statement and have an **open-minded approach**. The best answers suggest meanings and interpretations (plural):
>
> - What do you understand by the question? Is this theme or idea more important in one text than in another? Why? How?
> - What are the different ways that this question or aspect can be read or viewed?
> - Can you challenge the viewpoint, if there is one? If so, what evidence is there? How can you present it in a thoughtful, reflective way?

> **Express original or creative approaches** fluently:
>
> - This isn't about coming up with entirely new ideas, but you need to show that you're actively engaged with thinking about the question, not just reproducing random facts and information you have learned.
> - **Synthesise** your ideas – pull ideas and points together to create something fresh.
> - This is a linking/comparison response, so ensure that you guide your reader through your ideas logically, clearly and with professional language.

> **Know what to compare/contrast: form**, **structure** and **language** will **always** be central to your response, even where you also have to write about characters, contexts or culture.
>
> - Think about standard versus more conventional **narration** (for example, use of **foreshadowing**, disrupted time or narrative voice which leads to dislocation or difficulty in reading).
> - Consider different characteristic use of language: lengths of sentences, formal/informal style, **dialect**, accent, balance of dialogue and narration; the difference between forms, if appropriate (for example prose treatment of an idea and a play) or the different ways two novels use the possibilities offered by first person narrative.
> - Look at a variety of **symbols**, **images** and **motifs** (how they represent concerns of the author/time; what they are and how and where they appear; how they link to critical perspectives; their purposes, effects and impact on the novel).
> - Consider aspects of genres (to what extent do Charlotte Brontë and the author(s) of the other work(s) conform to/challenge/subvert particular genres or styles of writing?)

EXAMINER'S TIP ✓

Be sure to give due weight to each text – if there are two texts, this would normally mean giving them equal attention (but check the exact requirements of your task). Where required or suggested by the course you are following, you could try moving fluently between the texts in each paragraph, as an alternative to treating texts separately. This approach can be impressive and will ensure that comparison is central to your response.

WRITING YOUR RESPONSE

The depth and extent of your answer will depend on how much you have to write, but the key will be to **explore in detail**, and **link between ideas and texts**. Let us use the same example.

> Compare the depiction of female adolescence in *Jane Eyre* and other text(s) you have studied.

INTRODUCTION TO YOUR RESPONSE

- Briefly discuss what 'female adolescence' means, and how well this applies to your texts.
- Mention in support the importance of adolescence in *Jane Eyre* and the other text(s).
- You could begin with a powerful quotation that you use to launch into your response. For example, using Carter's *The Magic Toyshop*:

> *'Since she was thirteen, when her periods began' Melanie has felt 'pregnant with herself'. Jane is thirteen when she is locked in the red-room and experiences a crisis suggestive of the onset of menstruation. This is the age when both Jane and Melanie begin to become conscious of their bodies and in both novels the transition to sexual maturity plays a crucial role.*

MAIN BODY OF YOUR RESPONSE

- **Point 1:** start with the representation of female adolescence in *Jane Eyre* and what it tells us about the novel's themes. What is your view? Are the uses of adolescence similar in the other text(s)? Are there any relevant critical viewpoints that you know about? Are there contextual or cultural factors to consider?

- **Point 2:** now cover a new treatment or aspect through comparison or contrast of this theme in your other text(s). How is this treatment or aspect presented **differently or similarly** by the writer(s) in the language, form, structures used? Why was this done in this way? How does it reflect the writers' interests? What do the critics say? Are there contextual or cultural factors to consider?

- **Points 3, 4, 5, etc.:** address a range of other factors and aspects, for example the representation of characters apart from the **protagonists either** within *Jane Eyre* **or** in both *Jane Eyre* and another text. What different ways do you respond to these (with more empathy, greater criticism, less interest) – and why? For example:

> *Jane and Melanie are not the only characters whose emotional and psychic transformations are echoed in their bodies. Rochester proves that he has become a better husband and Christian when he is disfigured in the fire at Thornfield during the attempt to rescue his first wife.*

CONCLUSION

- Synthesise elements of what you have said into a final paragraph that fluently, succinctly and inventively leaves the reader/examiner with the sense that you have engaged with this task and the texts. For example:

> *Carter, Rhys and Brontë have each created worlds in which much is not what it seems. In each case, the reader is presented with a central female character of intense feeling who – at the point of her transition into womanhood – falls victim to patriarchal deceptions that she must struggle against in order to find herself. Antoinette's tragedy is that she never really achieves this except perhaps at the moment of her death. Jane's triumph is that, unencumbered by poverty, race or blighted marriage, she can act independently.*

> **EXAMINER'S TIP** ✓
>
> Be creative with your conclusion! It's the last thing the examiner will read and your chance to make your mark.

CHECK THE BOOK **A02**

Fred Botting in *Gothic* (1996) outlines the ways in which the **Gothic** genre was designed to create physical, i.e. sensational effects, in the reader, through excess. He says 'Gothic atmospheres – gloomy and mysterious – have repeatedly signalled the disturbing return of pasts upon presents and evoked emotions of terror' (p. 1).

EXAMINER'S TIP ✓

You may be asked to discuss the other text(s) you have studied as well as *Jane Eyre* as part of your response. Once you have completed your response on the novel you could move on to discuss the same issues in your other text(s). Begin with a simple linking phrase or sentence to launch straight into your first point about your next text, such as: *The supernatural is presented in a quite different way in "The Magic Toyshop".* Here,...

RESPONDING TO A GENERAL QUESTION ABOUT THE WHOLE TEXT

You may also be asked to write about a specific aspect of *Jane Eyre* – but as it relates to the **whole text**. For example:

> **Explore the use Charlotte Brontë makes of Gothic and supernatural elements in *Jane Eyre*.**

This means you should:

● Focus on the **Gothic *and* the supernatural elements specifically** (not *all* supernatural things).

● **Explain their use** – *how* they are used by Charlotte Brontë in terms of action, character and ideas or themes. Consider the conventions linked to them – the associations with night, the appearance of doubles, the cry in the night that calls Jane back to Rochester.

● Look at aspects of the **whole novel**, not just one chapter.

STRUCTURING YOUR RESPONSE

You need a clear, logical plan, as for all tasks that you do. It is impossible to write about every section or part of the text, so you will need to:

● Quickly note 5–6 key points or aspects to build your essay around:
Point a: *Jane sometimes experiences wild feelings and aberrant psychological states.*
Point b: *Jane wishes to go beyond the limits prescribed by her society.*
Point c: *These elements generate melodramatic and therefore sensational effects.*
Point d: *These elements move the plot forward at key moments.*
Point e: *Gothic and supernatural moments permeate the whole novel.*

● Then decide the most effective or logical order. For example, **point e**, then **c, a, d, b**, etc.

You could begin with your key or main idea, with supporting evidence/references, followed by your further points (perhaps two paragraphs for each). For example:

Paragraph 1: first key point: *The Gothic and supernatural permeate the whole novel, from Jane's apparent meeting with a ghost in the 'red-room' to her response to Rochester's eerie, pained cry of 'Jane! Jane! Jane!'*

Paragraph 2: expand out, link into other areas: *The supernatural and Gothic also underlie the scenes of greatest sensational effect, in which readers empathise with Jane's emotional state.*

Paragraph 3: change direction, introduce new aspect/point: *The sensational scenes focused on the experience of heightened feeling and aberrant psychological states enable Brontë to create powerful effects though both language and action, and to move the novel forward.* And so on.

● For your **conclusion:** use a compelling way to finish, perhaps repeating some or all of the key words from the question. For example you could end with:

Your final point, but with an additional clause which makes clear what you think is key to the question:
Jane's transformation by the end of the novel, from a young 'wild cat' to a woman who has a very clear sense of both 'principle' and 'judgment', enables Brontë to create a psychologically truthful climax to the depiction of unconscious states. Or:

A **new quotation** or **an aspect that's slightly different** from your main point:

The novel's final lines come from a letter written by St John, who says that his response to imminent death is '"even so come, Lord Jesus!"' which echoes Jane's response to Rochester's call to her in the night. The novel's total effect of defamiliarisation is therefore to make even conventional religious sentiment seem supernatural, which shocked nineteenth-century readers.

Or a combination of these endings.

WRITING ABOUT CONTEXTS

Assessment Objective 4 asks you to 'demonstrate understanding of the significance and influence of the contexts in which literary texts are written and received'. This can mean:

- How the events, settings, politics and so on **of the time when the text was written** influenced the writer or help us to understand the novel's themes or concerns. For example, to what extent Charlotte Brontë might have been influenced by arguments about religion in Victorian England.

or

- How events, settings, politics and so on **of the time when the text is read** influences how it is understood. For example, would readers reading the novel today see parallels between Jane's marginalisation and intensity of feeling and some aspects of modern understandings of those who experience living on the autism spectrum?

THE CONTEXT FOR *JANE EYRE*

You might find the following table of suggested examples helpful for thinking about how particular aspects of the time contribute to our understanding of the play and its themes. These are just examples – can you think of any others?

POLITICAL	LITERARY	PHILOSOPHICAL
Debates about education, industrial radicalism, Luddism, Chartism, New Poor Law 1834	Gothic, Bible, fairy tales and **folklore**, **Romanticism**, **Realism**	Reason, stoicism – Dr Johnson's *Rasselas*
SCIENTIFIC	**CULTURAL**	**SOCIAL**
Phrenology, Sir Humphrey Davy's *Elements of Chemistry* (1827), Berwick's *History of British Birds*	**Evangelicalism**, anti-Catholicism, imperialism and 'race'	Women's social position, plight of governesses, class, marriage laws, property relations, unemployment

TARGETING A HIGH GRADE   AO4

Remember that the extent to which you write about these contexts will be determined by the marks available. Some questions or tasks may have very few marks allocated for **AO4**, but where you do have to refer to context the key thing is not to 'bolt on' your comments, or write a long, separate chunk of text on context and then 'go back' to the novel. For example, **Don't** just write:

The 1830s was a time of widespread radicalism in England. Because of the development of industrial methods and increasing use of machinery, many working class men and women were deskilled or thrown out of work. Poverty and unemployment were commonplace and led to widespread revolt, especially after the New Poor Law was introduced in 1834. The Chartists sought a political voice through reform, but the Luddites and others took more direct action and smashed machinery. This political ferment seems to have provided the backdrop to the novel and religious controversies are important in the novel too.

Do write:

Charlotte Brontë's first audiences would have found echoes of both the social and religious controversies of their time in the novel. Jane attends Lowood school, and in each of her encounters with its Evangelical master establishes that his faith, and therefore his regime, are hypocritical. However, in the spirit of educational and social reform that is typical of the time, the school is inspected and re-established under a new and more rational system. As Jane continues her education there, so she acquires the accomplishments suitable to a young woman of her class, who would then – with no prospect of marriage – seek a career, as Jane does, as a governess.

> **EXAMINER'S TIP** ✓
>
> Remember that linking the historical, literary or social context to the novel is key to achieving the best marks for AO4.

USING CRITICAL INTERPRETATIONS AND PERSPECTIVES

THE 'MEANING' OF A TEXT

There are many viewpoints and perspectives on the 'meaning' of *Jane Eyre*, and examiners will be looking for evidence that you have considered a range of these. Broadly speaking, these different interpretations might relate to the following considerations:

1. CHARACTER

What **sort/type** of person Jane – or another character – is:

- Is the character an **'archetype'** (a specific type of character with common features)? *Sandra M. Gilbert and Susan Gubar see Jane as a definitive female figure who seeks 'escape-into-wholeness'. In this, she might be compared with other rebellious spirits, such Shakespeare's Desdemona, though …*
- Does the character **personify**, **symbolise** or represent a specific idea (for example, rebellion and revolt, the inner battle between passion and self-control, romantic wish-fulfilment)?
- Is the character modern, universal, of his/her time, historically accurate, etc.? Can we see aspects of Jane's rebellious thinking, which refuses to accept social mores and customs, in public figures (such as public intellectuals or campaigners) from our own time?

2. IDEAS AND ISSUES

What the novel tells us about **particular ideas** or **issues** and how we can interpret these. For example:

- The importance of faith
- Passion vs. restraint
- What weight to give to the self
- Moral and social codes, etc.

3. LINKS AND CONTEXTS

To what extent the novel **links with, follows or pre-echoes** other texts and/or ideas. For example:

- Its influence culturally, historically and socially (do we see echoes of the characters or genres in other texts?) How like Jane is Melanie from *The Magic Toyshop*, and why? Does the novel share features with **Romantic** or **Gothic** fiction?
- How its language links to other texts or modes, such as religious works, **folklore**, fairy tale, etc.

4. NARRATIVE STRUCTURE

How the novel is **constructed** and how Charlotte Brontë **makes** her **narrative**:

- Does it follow a particular narrative convention, such as the 'coming of age' story?
- What is the function of specific events, characters, settings, etc. in relation to the narrative?
- What are the specific moments of tension, conflict, crisis and **denouement** – and do we agree on what they are?

5. READER RESPONSE

How the novel **works on a reader**, and whether this changes over time and in different contexts:

- Are we to empathise with, feel distance from, judge and/or evaluate the events and characters?

6. CRITICAL REACTION

And finally, how different readers view the novel: for example, different **critics over time**, or different **readers** in **earlier or more recent years**.

WRITING ABOUT CRITICAL PERSPECTIVES

The important thing to remember is that **you** are a critic too. Your job is to evaluate what a critic or school of criticism has said about these elements, and arrive at your own conclusions.

In essence, you need to: **consider** the views of others, **synthesise** them, then decide on **your perspective**. For example:

EXPLAIN THE VIEWPOINTS

Critical view A about Jane's desire to be whole:

> *Sandra M. Gilbert and Susan Gubar argue that in Thornfield's attic and on its battlements 'Jane's own rationality' and 'her irrationality intersect'. In close physical proximity to Bertha Rochester at these moments, and hearing her laugh, Jane seeks her 'own secret self'.*

Critical view B about Jane's desire to be whole:

> *During the incident in the 'red-room' Jane mis- or fails to recognise herself in the mirror, seeing instead, like Rochester later, a 'half fairy, half imp'. This first sight of herself sets up a project, Susannah B. Mintz argues, for Jane to learn how to 'manoeuvre between subject positions' without collapsing these into an 'orderly, unstrange whole'.*

THEN SYNTHESISE AND ADD YOUR PERSPECTIVE

Synthesise these views whilst adding your own:

> *Feminist readings have frequently stressed the relationship that exists between 'Jane and herself'. But, more recently, critics have said that the moment at which Jane fails to recognise herself in the mirror in the 'red-room' is not, as Gilbert and Gubar argued, significant because we see her projecting her frustrations into the mirror, rather it offers the radical possibility of sustaining contradictions and strangeness. This is persuasive. What she sees in the mirror is certainly evidence of her anger and inner battle to see herself as the Reeds see her. Her wholeness – and Rochester's wholeness in another way – remains unresolved, her selves in tension, throughout the remainder of the novel. And on this point critics agree. But, it does not then necessarily follow that Jane seeks to integrate what she sees into herself, to make herself whole in the ways that the Victorian reader might have expected, or that the revelation of the split, in and of itself, is key.*
>
> *I feel that it is more satisfactory to read the novel as a study of a protagonist who shows us that it is possible to be accepted for herself: both strange, and a heroine …*

CRITICAL VIEWPOINT **A03**

> 'We tend today to think of *Jane Eyre* as moral gothic, … *Pamela*'s daughter and *Rebecca*'s aunt, the archetypal scenario for all those mildly thrilling romantic encounters between a scowling Byronic hero (who owns a gloomy mansion) and a trembling heroine (who can't quite figure out the mansion's floor plan).' (Sandra M. Gilbert and Susan Gubar, *The Madwoman in the Attic: The Woman Writer and the Nineteenth-Century Literary Imagination* (1979), p. 337.)

ANNOTATED SAMPLE ANSWERS

Below are extracts from two sample answers to the same question at different grades. Bear in mind that these are examples only, covering all four Assessment Objectives – you will need to check the type of question and the weightings given for the four AOs when writing your coursework essay or practising for your exam.

> 'Charlotte Brontë presents Jane as a liberated character when in fact she is just as imprisoned by her class and gender as every other woman in the text.' How far do you agree with this description of Jane?

CANDIDATE 1

The period in which "Jane Eyre" was written was one of major social and political upheaval. The Chartists were trying to get the vote for the working man, and were not the only ones to rebel, the Luddites had responded to the introduction of machinery by breaking the machines. Charlotte Brontë, who lived in the North of England, would have been well aware of these rebellions. Jane is in sympathy with the 'millions' who protest either silently or visibly in 'political rebellions'. But, Jane never escapes the prison of her class or her gender.

> **AO4** Good introduction of context, though not strictly relevant, should be picked up again later

What is Jane Eyre's class? At the beginning she is not really part of the Reed family – she is looked down on by her aunt as not belonging to the same social class as her three cousins. She is next sent to an 'institution' – Lowood is a charitable school – and later has to work as a governess, which is when she takes the job at Thornfield. As a governess she then looks down on the other servants, even those who are kind to her. In the end, she is able to marry Rochester only because she inherits a fortune – so, nothing changes.

> **AO4** Shows how social class could exist within a finely balanced set of relationships, but could have developed point about peculiar position of governesses

> **AO2** Simplistic analysis, without supporting examples; does not demonstrate a good knowledge of the text

> **AO2** Refers to the structure of the novel, and its plotting, but does not really analyse it and a little unclear

Jane is also limited because she is a Victorian woman. Jane must be 'respectable'. Without owning anything, all that she can do is marry. If she allows herself to become Rochester's mistress, when she knows he already has a wife, she will lose everything. In fact, it seems that if she did do this she would become a lunatic like Bertha. All Rochester seems to want, until he meets Jane, is mistresses, and then he wants her to become one as well. He is like Bluebeard. However, because she sets him a good example, she does the right thing and she is moral like a good Victorian woman should be. Later, she seems to be rewarded because the Rivers family save her and then she inherits too. In the end, Rochester does the right thing too by trying to save Bertha – but he is hurt and she dies. Because of all of this, Rochester and Jane can in the end do what they want, marry and have children, which some critics have said is a conventional ending.

> **AO2** Good observation that this is implied, but no reference to supporting material

> **AO3** Good point about property, but it would have been strengthened by reference to appropriate critics

> **AO3** A good observation about Bluebeard, but not followed through

> **AO1** Simple summary, not argument

> **AO3** Gestures towards recognition that critics have discussed the issues raised by the question, but does not develop the point

In fact, all of the women in "Jane Eyre" are imprisoned by

A02 Useful point but misses opportunity to use quotation

A03 Demonstrates awareness of readers' original responses

their class and gender. Servants can only watch, because they are working class. Women must marry – the only young woman who does not marry becomes a nun! Despite Jane's desire to escape her class and sex, and despite readers' shocked responses to the novel, which saw Jane as very rebellious, even as unchristian, Jane in fact remains imprisoned by her class and gender like every other woman in the text. I do not believe that she is liberated at all.

A02 Interesting point attempted in describing other characters' situations but no reference to names

A01 Attempts to address key point in question, but point clumsily made. Rather circular

Comment

A01 Expression, though sometimes lacking fluency, is mostly clear. Addresses the topic but tends to deal with 'class' and 'gender' separately with little synthesis and there is little attention to Jane's experience as compared to any 'other woman in the text'.

A02 There is a fairly sustained response to the bounds of 'class' and 'gender', though it isn't much developed beyond a narrative of what is obviously present in the novel. There are only a few, mostly implicit, comments on language and no detailed textual commentary although the answer does have a few helpful integrated quotations.

A03 There is little consideration of alternative interpretations, though there is awareness that they might need to be addressed

A04 There is some contextual detail in the first paragraph, which addresses the question of what it might mean to be 'liberated', but this is not integrated into the remainder of the essay or returned to. Comes close to simply dropping historical and biographical material into the start of the essay and not returning to it. There is some awareness of ways different audiences might react.

For a B grade
To gain a higher grade, the answers would need to include at least some of the following:

A01 Tighter focus on the argument and more consideration of relevant alternative interpretations

A02 Developed account of narrative form and structure with attention to language, including more integrated quotation from the text

A04 Better use of contextual factors directly relevant to the question.

CANDIDATE 2

A03 Makes use of established criticism

A01 Well expressed and appropriately scholarly

A03 Stays focused on the question, good synthesis of key issues and use of critical perspective

A04 Draws on contextual material to build an argument

A02 Uses literary critical terms with precision

A02 Good point on form and structure, supported from the text

A03 Cites parallel texts and rewriting

Charlotte Brontë was of the class and gender that she depicts Jane as belonging to and, ever since Mrs Gaskell's seminal "The Life of Charlotte Brontë" (1857) much of her own life is said to have been reflected by Jane's story. But, well aware of the limits placed on women in her position by her society, especially governesses, Brontë in my view knew very well that the novel was not, as Jane herself says 'a regular autobiography'. Instead it's a Bildungsroman written as if by Jane a number of years after events have passed and therefore giving her time for mature reflection. "Jane Eyre" both presents the reader with the facts with reference to the position of Victorian middle class women and appears to offer a real imaginative exploration of the possibility, costs and rewards of stepping over the limits.

As a Bildungsroman, "Jane Eyre" is a 'coming of age' story. It is about the protagonist's progress from childhood to maturity and the struggle to find identity. That struggle, for a young woman limited by the demands of class and gender, is represented as painful, and Jane stops to pass comment and addresses us directly in the moments of most passionate feeling generated by the checks placed on her by her social position – moments such as that when she leaves Thornfield. 'Gentle reader,' she says, after subjecting herself to the demands of propriety as a property-less young woman, 'may you never feel what I then felt!'

Jane must, it seems, follow the social conventions in order to maintain her respectability, which as Marxist feminist critics have observed is the only commodity she has. Ultimately, having behaved properly, having suppressed her passionate desire for Rochester, she marries well, which her class and gender suggest she ought to do. In this way, she might appear to live a life as restricted as any of the other young middling women who play a part in the novel, women such as Diana and Mary Rivers, and Georgiana Reed who all also marry successfully – Diana and Mary because Jane has given them money and therefore the freedom to marry for love. Even the servant Bessie marries well, in her own way in her own class.

However, Jane's story is in my view unconventional, as Brontë's deliberate use of fairy tale suggests. Like Cinderella she is liberated from the bonds of service and marries above herself, like Little Red Riding Hood she escapes the wolf, like feminist versions of Bluebeard she finds out her master's secrets, but escapes her predecessors' horrible end.

AO3 Draws on appropriate critical responses

Jane, if not quite liberated, I would argue at least manages to avoid the potential pitfalls of her passionate nature and go back to reclaim what she most desires having quite literally thrown off the most repressive hand in the book (that of St John Rivers as he proposes). As Gilbert and Gubar have observed, she is quite discordant within her family, and in her society, (an 'imp' as she observes of herself in the 'red-room'), and we see this most clearly when she stands on the battlements of Thornfield and aches to have the freedom to see and experience the wider world – a desire expressed through the use of Chartist-like language, the language of rebellion: 'Millions' and 'masses'. It was this that made Victorian readers react as if the novel were almost a radical tract, a lesson in successful revolt. Though Jane might be said to be as trapped by class and gender as the other women in the novel, her strangeness sets her apart and allows the reader the liberty to make the ordinary seem unfamiliar, and so question the dominant codes of class and gender.

AO4 Argument supported by appropriate contextual material

AO3 Considers changing reader responses

GRADE A

The student moves on to consider the unconventional aspects of Jane's relationship with Rochester ...

Comment

AO1 There is a clear sense from the opening that the candidate has a grasp of the whole text and of the question. The answer is shaped by an overview which links together incidents throughout the novel and each paragraph moves the argument forward.

AO2 The response keeps a tight focus on whether or not one may agree with the statement, with a number of telling details about structure and form. Textual evidence is provided for a number of points about Brontë's use of language; quotations are neatly integrated into the discussion.

AO3 There are several indications of alternative interpretations, either through criticism or through reader responses. The connection to feminist readings is effective.

AO4 The question is illuminated by a number of contextual references which address both the construction of the text itself and the ways readers in different periods and with different perspectives may respond.

For an A* grade

To gain a higher grade, the answer might include at least some of the following:

AO2 A closer look at one or two detailed examples of the ways the language and form are used to present the elements of class and gender.

AO2 Further consideration of ways in which the structure of the novel enhances the sense of tension between the operation of social constraint and the need to be true to the self, as hinted at in the references to wholeness.

AO3 More developed consideration of alternative readings or creative revisions of the question of a woman's place in society, for example, by reference to feminist rewriting or critical responses.

AO4 Further exploration of the ways in which the context in which the novel was written and has been read could affect the topic.

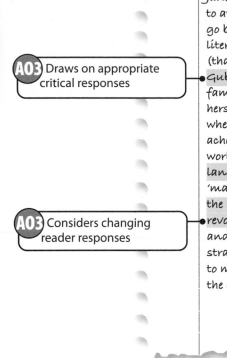

WORKING THROUGH A TASK

Now it's your turn to work through a task on *Jane Eyre*. The key is to:

- Read/decode the task/question.
- Plan your points – then expand and link your points.
- Draft your answer.

TASK TITLE

How far do you agree with the idea that Charlotte Brontë portrays Jane's story as a love story?

DECODE THE QUESTION: KEY WORDS

How far do you agree..?   = what are **my** views?

Brontë portrays   = a reminder that this is a literary creation

love story   = romantic **narrative** or quest

Jane's story   = narrative focused on a central **protagonist**

PLAN AND EXPAND

- Key aspect: evidence of 'love story'?

POINT	POINT EXPANDED	EVIDENCE
Point a *The narrative contains moments of intense feeling and passion appropriate to a love story.*	*In Chapter XXIII Rochester proposes marriage, and in her responses to his preamble – in which he typically dances around the subject to test Jane – Jane's sadness at the potential loss of the man she loves, despite propriety, prevents her speaking. However, in the preamble we also see the foreshadowing of the failure of this attempt to marry, and the dangers to Jane if she should succumb to bigamy.*	Rochester: "'you'd forget me." "That I never should, sir: you know –" Impossible to proceed.' (Chapter XXIII, p. 291) Rochester: "'I shall myself look out for … an asylum for you.'" (Chapter XXIII, p. 290)
Point b *Governess falls in love with her employer, who seeks to marry her. Though initially there are obstacles in their way, in the end they are united.*	Different aspects of this point expanded You fill in	Quotations 1–2 You fill in
Point c *There are parallels between this and fairy stories like 'Cinderella' or 'Beauty and the Beast'.*	Different aspects of this point expanded You fill in	Quotations 1–2 You fill in

- Key aspect: evidence of 'Jane's story'

POINT	POINT EXPANDED	EVIDENCE
Point a You fill in	Different aspects of this point expanded You fill in	Quotations 1–2 You fill in
Point b You fill in	Different aspects of this point expanded You fill in	Quotations 1–2 You fill in
Point c You fill in	Different aspects of this point expanded You fill in	Quotations 1–2 You fill in

CONCLUSION

POINT	POINT EXPANDED	EVIDENCE
Key final point or overall view *You fill in*	Draw together and perhaps add a final further point to support your view *You fill in*	Final quotation to support your view *You fill in*

DEVELOP FURTHER AND DRAFT

Now look back over your draft points and:

- Add further links or connections between the points to develop them further or synthesise what has been said, for example:

> *As Gilbert and Gubar have argued, it is easy to see Jane's story as a romantic encounter with a Byronic hero. However, despite Brontë's deliberate use of fairy-tale structures, in which Jane's finally marrying Rochester appears to reprise Cinderella's story, the narrative cannot be reduced to this level …*

- Decide an order for your points/paragraphs – some may now be linked/connected and therefore **not** in the order of the table on the page opposite.

Now draft your essay. If you're really stuck you can use the opening paragraph below to get you started.

> *The novel opens with a depiction of Jane's family life that makes it quite clear that she is a 'discord in Gateshead Hall': orphaned, friendless and living without experiencing kindness or care. At its conclusion she attends her husband compassionately; he loves her 'so truly' that neither is shamed by his need. Jane's journey is one, like Cinderella's, that moves from margin to centre and brings her true love. Yet, the novel is not a love story …*

Once you've written your essay, turn to page 111 for a mark scheme on this question to see how well you've done.

FURTHER QUESTIONS

1. What seems to make Jane so unacceptable to her 'superiors'?
2. To what extent is Charlotte Brontë attacking **Evangelicalism** in *Jane Eyre*?
3. Compare and contrast the characterisation of St John Rivers with that of Rochester.
4. To what extent does the representation of female desire in *Jane Eyre* challenge mid-nineteenth-century notions of morality and femininity?
5. Given the fairy-tale aspect of the plotting, to what extent is the novel convincing?
6. Why might it be necessary for Rochester to be blinded and physically impaired before he and Jane can finally be united?
7. How does Jane's relationship with Bessie change and what does this reveal about Jane herself?
8. How does the **narrative** structure of *Jane Eyre* compare to other **Realist** novels?
9. Consider the ways in which Thornfield's architecture represents Jane's psychological state and its master's condition.
10. In what ways does Charlotte Brontë draw on classic literary forms and genres, such as **Romantic** literature or the **Gothic**?

ESSENTIAL STUDY TOOLS

FURTHER READING

BIOGRAPHY

P. Boumelha, *Charlotte Brontë*, Harvester, New York and London, 1990
An excellent biography

Elizabeth Gaskell, *The Life of Charlotte Brontë*, Everyman, London, first published 1857, 1998
The first major biography. Very influential

L. Miller, *The Brontë Myth*, Vintage, London, 2002
How we've come to see the Brontës as we do

T. J. Wise & J. A. Symington (eds), *The Brontës, their Lives, Friendships and Correspondence*, Blackwell, Oxford, 1933
Standard reference work, includes many of the Brontë's letters

LITERARY CRITICISM

D. Bolt, J. M. Rodas, and E. J. Donaldson, (eds) *The Madwoman and the Blindman: Jane Eyre, Discourse, Disability*, Ohio State University Press, Ohio, 2012
Critical essays from a disability studies approach

C. Brontë, *Jane Eyre*, Penguin, London, 1966
An interesting introduction by Q. D. Leavis

T. Eagleton, *Myths of Power: A Marxist Study of the Brontës*, Macmillan, Basingstoke, 1975
Marxist reading

S. M. Gilbert and S. Gubar, *The Madwoman in the Attic: The Woman Writer and the Nineteenth-Century Literary Imagination*, Yale University Press, Newhaven and London, 1979
Discusses the relationship of the author to the subject

E. Imlay, *Charlotte Brontë and the Mysteries of Love: Myth and Allegory in Jane Eyre*, Harvester Wheatsheaf, New York, London, 1989
A study of the imagery used in the novel

Tony Tanner, 'Passion, Narrative and Identity in *Wuthering Heights* and *Jane Eyre*' in *Contemporary Approaches to Narrative*, ed. Anthony Mortimer, Tübingen, 1984
A valuable survey of some of the key issues

HISTORICAL CONTEXT

L. Davidoff and C. Hall, *Family Fortunes: Men and Women of the English Middle Class 1780–1850*, 2nd edn, Routledge, London, 2002
An excellent history of the period

Inga-Stina Ewbank, *Their Proper Sphere, A Study of the Brontë Sisters as Early-Victorian Female Novelists*, Edward Arnold, London, 1996
Places the Brontës in their historical context

M. Poovey, *Uneven Developments: The Ideological Work of Gender in Mid-Victorian England*, University of Chicago Press, Chicago, 1988
Discusses the history of governesses

S. Shuttleworth, *Charlotte Brontë and Victorian Psychology*, Cambridge University Press, Cambridge, 1996
Includes a discussion of phrenology

M. Thormahlen, *The Brontës and Religion*, Cambridge University Press, Cambridge, 1999
Detailed study, particularly of Anglicanism

LITERARY CONTEXT

B. Ashcroft, G. Griffiths and H. Tiffin, *The Empire Writes Back: Theory and Practice in Post-Colonial Literatures*, Routledge, London, 2002
Postcolonial reading

Fred Botting, *Gothic*, Routledge, London and New York, 1996
A useful introduction to the genre

Lord David Cecil, *Early Victorian Novelists: essays in revaluation*, Constable, London, 1934
Traditional take on the subject

E. Figes, *Sex and Subterfuge: Women Writers to 1850*, Pandora, London, 1982
Complex feminist readings of texts

H. Fraser with D. Brown, *English Prose of the Nineteenth Century*, Longman, London, 1996
Good contextual survey

R. Gilmour, *The Victorian Period: The Intellectual and Cultural Context of English Literature 1830–1890*, Longman, London, 1993
Good contextual survey

P. Hulme, *Colonial Discourse/Postcolonial Theory*, Manchester University Press, Manchester, 1994
Postcolonial reading

David Lodge, *The Art of Fiction*, Penguin, London, 1992
Each chapter concentrates on one aspect of fiction

E. Said, *Orientalism*, Routledge and Kegan Paul, London, 1978
Postcolonial reading

Elaine Showalter, *A Literature of Their Own*, Princeton University Press, Princeton, N. J., 1977
Women's writing in the nineteenth century

G. C. Spivak, *Critical Inquiry* 12:1 (1985)
Postcolonial reading

N. D. Thompson, *Reviewing Sex Gender and the Reception of Victorian Novels*, Macmillan, Basingstoke, 1996
Includes discussion of the reception of *Jane Eyre*

R. Williams, *The English Novel from Dickens to Lawrence*, Chatto & Windus, London, 1970
Seminal literary criticism

R. Williams, *Keywords: A Vocabulary of Culture and Society*, Fontana, London, 1988
A useful history of language

BACKGROUND READING

Mary Braddon, *Lady Audley's Secret*, Wordsworth Editions Ltd., Ware, first edition 1862, 1997
Very popular Victorian sensation novel

A. Carter, *The Bloody Chamber*, Penguin, London, 1981
Includes a rewriting of 'Bluebeard'

A. Carter (ed.), *The Virago Book of Fairy Tales*, Virago, London, 1990

A. Carter (ed.), *The Second Book of Virago Fairy Tales*, Virago, London, 1992
Classic versions of fairy stories

M. Humm, *Border Traffic Strategies of Contemporary Women Writers*, Manchester University Press, Manchester, 1991
Complex feminist reading of *Wide Sargasso Sea*

Jean Rhys, *Wide Sargasso Sea*, Penguin, London, first edition 1966, 2000
A rewriting of Bertha Mason's story

LITERARY TERMS

analogy illustration of an idea by means of a more familiar idea that is similar or parallel to it in some way

archetype a specific type of character with common features

asceticism a discipline of self-imposed austerity and abstinence for spiritual improvement

Bildungsroman is a 'coming of age' story, a novel describing the progress of a character from childhood to maturity that focuses on the relationship between character, experience, education and identity. The Bildungsroman can be seen as a kind of underground confessional writing, which emerged at the turn of the eighteenth to nineteenth centuries. Other examples include Dickens's *David Copperfield* and *Great Expectations*

colloquialism everyday speech used by people in informal situations

defamiliarisation the effect of making the familiar seem unfamiliar

denouement the final unfolding of the plot

dialect a manner of speaking or form of language peculiar to an individual or particular region or class; it differs from the standard language of a country

Evangelicalism from the Greek *evangelion* ('good news' or 'Gospel'), in the Brontës' day related to the Evangelical Movement, an early nineteenth-century Christian movement which sought to reform the Anglican Church

Exposition (adj. **expository**) an explanation or to do with the delivery of information. Authors often use exposition to set the scene, but will tend to try and disguise it in order to maintain the reader's belief in the world that is being created. Information is therefore often smuggled in through conversation and other means

foil a contrast achieved by putting an inferior example alongside a more impressive one

folklore traditional stories and legends, which sometimes give rise to received wisdom or custom

foreshadowing giving a sign of something to come

Gothic Gothic novels are fictions that deal with cruel passions and supernatural terrors in some medieval setting, such as a haunted house or monastery. Gothic novels often rely on **defamiliarisation** for their effects. In their depiction of wild feelings they are both precursors and part of the literary movement called **Romanticism**. Works with a similarly obsessive, gloomy, violent and spine-chilling atmosphere, but not necessarily with a medieval setting, are also called Gothic. Indeed, any work concentrating on the bizarre, the macabre or aberrant psychological states may be called Gothic

imagery an image, at its most basic, is a word-picture but in literary discussion it is used to denote the terms in which an object or person or action is described to make the described thing more vivid in the reader's mind. The most obvious examples of an image are metaphor and simile. Imagery is the collective or repeated use of such imaginative or figurative presentations of things; it can be employed for all of the terms which refer to objects and qualities and which appeal to the senses and the feelings

irony a form of sarcasm. Saying one thing and meaning another. A norm is established and then subverted

journalistic short, terse and sometimes informal written style like that found in a newspaper

melodrama (adj.**melodramatic**) a genre of drama which aims to excite through incident and strong but simple feelings, with clearly 'good' or 'bad' characters and a happy ending

metaphor a departure from literal writing which goes further than a comparison between two different things or ideas by fusing them together: one thing is described as being another thing, thus 'carrying over' all its associations

morality play an allegory in which the forces of good and evil and a Christian moral lesson concerning salvation are dramatised with simplicity and vigour

motif a recurring idea in a work, which is used to draw the reader's attention to a particular theme or topic

narrative a story, tale or any recital of events, and the manner in which it is told

narrator the voice telling the story or relating a sequence of events

Neoclassicism the generalised beliefs of Neoclassical writers are based on the premise that the world is God's carefully ordered creation, with 'man' as a rational being capable of living harmoniously in society. Man's rational intelligence was honoured and valued above all other faculties. Reason demonstrated that the great truths about the world were well known, and fixed: the writer's duty was to express these truths in appropriate language. Unlike **Romantics**, Neoclassical writers did not value creativity or originality highly

Orient English-speakers in the Victorian period often referred to India as 'the Orient'

pathetic fallacy the attribution of human feelings to objects in nature and, commonly, weather systems, so that the mood of the **narrator** or the characters can be discerned from the behaviour of the surrounding environment

pathos suffering feeling; that quality in a work of art that arouses pity and sadness

personification figurative language in which ideas, feelings or things are treated as if they were human beings

physiognomy study of the physical presentation of the face and head to determine an individual's character, morality and intellect. A respectable and established (pseudo)-science in the first half of the nineteenth century

protagonist the principal character in a work of literature

Realism a Realist author represents the world as it is rather than as it should be, using description rather than invention; observes and documents everyday life in straightforward prose; draws on characters from all levels of society, but often from the lowest classes and represents their speech and manners accurately. Realism became the dominant form of literature in the nineteenth century

Romantic novels of the Romantic period are concerned with valuing feelings and emotion rather than the human capacity to reason. They are also interested in trying to explain a person's living relationship with the world around them including nature, landscape and their imagination

saga prose narrative recounting heroic exploits

sublime quality of awesome grandeur, as distinguished from the beautiful, in nature

symbolism investing material objects with abstract powers and meanings greater than their own; allowing a complex idea to be represented by a single object

TIMELINE

WORLD EVENTS	CHARLOTTE'S LIFE	LITERARY EVENTS
1811 First Luddite riot, Nottingham		
	1812 Patrick Brontë, an Irish Protestant clergyman marries Maria Branwell, a Cornish Methodist from Penzance	
1813–17 Luddites executed, York. Movement broken	**1813** Birth of Maria	**1813** Jane Austen, *Pride and Prejudice*
	1813–18 Patrick publishes a collection of poems and two novels	
1815 Napoleon escapes from Elba, becomes Emperor and is defeated at Waterloo	**1815** Birth of Elizabeth	**1815** Byron, *Complete Works*
	1816 Birth of Charlotte	**1816** Jane Austen, *Emma*
	1817 Birth of Branwell	**1817** Death of Jane Austen
	1818 Birth of Emily	**1818** Mary Shelley, *Frankenstein*
1820 Death of George III (end of Regency), and accession of George IV, who attempts to dissolve his marriage to Caroline. Death of Napoleon	**1820** Birth of Anne. The Brontë family move to Haworth in Yorkshire	
	1821 Mrs Maria Brontë dies of cancer, and her sister, Elizabeth Branwell, comes to care for the children	**1821** Death of poet, John Keats
		1824 Death of poet, Lord Byron
1825 First railway opened between Stockton and Darlington	**1825** Both Maria and Elizabeth die of tuberculosis at Cowan Bridge School	
1829 Catholic emancipation in Britain		
1830 Death of George IV and accession of William IV		
1830s Abolitionists of Slave Trade active in America; articles in *Monthly Repository* by W. J. Fox and W. B. Adams influenced by Harriet Taylor		
1831 Cholera epidemic	**1831** Charlotte boards at Roe Head School, Mirfield	
1832 First Reform Act		**1832** Death of Walter Scott and Goethe; Harriet Martineau, *Illustrations of Political Economy*; Anna Jameson, *Characteristics of Women*
1833 Slavery abolished		
1834 Establishment of Union Workhouses; Tolpuddle Martyrs		
	1835–8 Charlotte returns to Roe Head as a teacher, with Emily as a pupil, but after three months of homesickness Emily returns to Haworth	
		1836 Charles Dickens, *The Pickwick Papers*
1837 Death of William IV; accession of Queen Victoria		
1838 'People's Charter' published		
1839 Chartist petition rejected by Parliament – riots, Birmingham	**1839** Charlotte, now a governess, visits Norton Conyers, near Rippon, model for Thornfield Hall. Charlotte turns down two proposals of marriage from her friend Ellen Nussey's clergyman brother, and from an Irish clergyman	

WORLD EVENTS	CHARLOTTE'S LIFE	LITERARY EVENTS
1840 Penny Post established		**1840** Death of novelist, Fanny Burney
	1841 Charlotte becomes governess to a family near Bradford	
1842 Second Chartist petition presented and rejected	**1842** Charlotte and Emily study French in Brussels at Mme Heger's school	
	1843 Charlotte returns to Brussels to teach and falls in love with Monsieur Heger	**1843** Margaret Fuller (American journalist), 'The Great Lawsuit – Man versus Men. Woman versus Women', *The Dial*
	1844 Charlotte returns home when her father becomes almost totally blind	
1845 Newman converts to the Catholic faith; Famine in Ireland due to potato blight		**1845** Margaret Fuller, *Women in the Nineteenth Century*
1846 Repeal of Corn Laws	**1846** *Poems by Currer, Ellis and Acton Bell* are published by the three sisters	**1846** Margaret Fuller visits Britain
	1847 Charlotte's *Jane Eyre* is published under the pseudonym of Currer Bell; Anne's *Agnes Grey* is published under the pseudonym of Acton Bell; Emily's *Wuthering Heights* is published under the pseudonym of Ellis Bell	**1847** William Thackeray, *Vanity Fair* (serialisation)
1848 Final Chartist petition rejected. Revolutions in Paris, Berlin, Vienna, Venice, Rome, Milan, Naples, Prague and Budapest; Marx and Engel, *Communist Manifesto*	**1848** Anne's *The Tenant of Wildfell Hall* is published; Branwell dies of alcoholism; Emily dies of tuberculosis	**1848** Elizabeth Gaskell, *Mary Barton*
1849 Cholera epidemic	**1849** Anne dies of tuberculosis, leaving Charlotte as the only surviving sibling. Charlotte publishes *Shirley*	**1849–54** *Eliza Cook's Journal*
	1849–51 Charlotte visits London and meets writers of her day: Mrs Gaskell, Harriet Martineau, William Thackeray	
1851 The Great Exhibition at the Crystal Palace		**1851** Harriet Taylor 'Enfranchisement of Women', in *Westminster Review*
		1852 Harriet Beecher Stowe, *Uncle Tom's Cabin*
	1853 Charlotte publishes *Villette*, based on her experiences in Brussels	
1854 Cholera epidemic	**1854** Charlotte marries her father's curate, Arthur Nicholls	
	1855 Charlotte is pregnant, but dies from a combination of ill health and pneumonia, before reaching full term	

REVISION FOCUS TASK ANSWERS

TASK 1

Consider the importance of religion in *Jane Eyre*.

- Mr Brocklehurst's zeal and religious professions, which are often contradictory and seem self-deceiving at best
- St John's **Evangelical** faith, religious practice and determination to be a missionary
- Miss Reed's move towards Catholicism and religious seclusion
- Helen Burns's stoicism
- Jane Eyre's development of religious faith, from childhood to adulthood

Consider the role of property and class in *Jane Eyre*.

- Jane's position at Gateshead, her education within a charitable institution, her need for respectable employment after she has finished school, her insistence that the Rivers family are offering her hospitality not charity
- The portrayal of working-class characters such as Bessie, Mrs Fairfax and the butler who tells Jane what has happened to Thornfield
- The dramatic change in Jane's position once she inherits – and the difference that this also makes to her female cousins (Rivers)

TASK 2

How far do you agree with the following statement: Landscape, place and nature carry character in *Jane Eyre*.

- The ways in which the weather and seasons add stress to mood and feeling in the novel – the **pathetic fallacy**
- The very close links between Thornfield and its master – the destruction of the tree after the storm that follows Rochester's proposal, the scarring of the house and of Mr Rochester following the fire
- The bleakness of the landscape through which Jane travels when looking for help after leaving Thornfield

How far do you agree with the following statement: In *Jane Eyre* disability is a real as well as a metaphorical condition.

- Bertha Mason/Rochester's 'madness', its causes, its effects and the way in which she is cared for
- Mr Rochester's injuries, caused by the fire at Thornfield, and their long-term impact
- The idea of a 'cure' within Victorian depictions of disability and redemption, often characterised as the 'school of pain'

TASK 3

How far do you agree with the following statement: Jane Eyre is a reliable narrator.

- We see everything from Jane Eyre's point of view, but at times the narrator points out that her writing is about her young self, by her older self.
- We get corroboration from two minor characters: Bessie and Mrs Fairfax, who are given authority within the text to support what Jane says.
- We may doubt Jane's narrative at times, e.g. regarding her jealousy of Miss Ingram. Also, we occasionally see Jane from another's point of view, e.g. her aunt's, at which time Jane becomes stranger and more alien to us.

How far do you agree with the following statement: Mr Rochester and St John Rivers are opposites.

- Each man represents one aspect of Jane's character. St John is **symbolic** of the aspect of Jane's character that wants to adhere to convention. Mr Rochester the side of her that is fiery and passionate.
- There are contrasting descriptions of their physical appearance: Rochester is heavy and dark; St John is handsome and fair.
- Rochester brings Jane alive; St John she feels is a deadening weight on her spirit.

TASK 4

Consider the importance of fairy tales in *Jane Eyre*.

- Fairy tales are introduced through the character of the servant Bessie; it was a commonplace in **Gothic** fiction for nursemaids to introduce their characters to the supernatural, and *Jane Eyre* contains many aspects of the Gothic form.
- There are a number of fairy tales that seem to be referenced in the novel: 'Cinderella' (Jane the orphan is a marginalised compared to her two female cousins at Gateshead, just as Cinderella is compared to her stepsisters; at the end she marries her prince and rises in the world); 'Bluebeard' (Jane must stay away from a locked room within Thornfield; the locked room contains a shocking secret and Rochester's wife); 'Beauty and the Beast' (Jane falls in love with the undesirable Rochester and they marry).
- Jane is often referred to as being like a sprite or a fairy by Rochester.

Consider the importance of dreams and the supernatural for prefiguring events in *Jane Eyre*.

- Dreams often seem to come true in *Jane Eyre*; as well as revealing powerful emotional forces at work, they also **foreshadow** later events.
- At times of heightened emotion, Jane experiences supernatural events, which move the narrative forward, or reveal important information to the reader.
- When Jane is locked in the red-room, she sees her uncle's ghost.
- Jane hears Rochester calling to her and this precipitates her return to Thornfield.

MARK SCHEME

Use this page to assess your answer to the Worked task, provided on page 104.

Aiming for an A grade? Fulfil all the criteria below and your answer should hit the mark.

> **How far do you agree with the idea that Charlotte Brontë portrays Jane's story as a love story?**

A01 — Articulate creative, informed and relevant responses to literary texts, using appropriate terminology and concepts, and coherent, accurate written expression.

- You make a range of clear, relevant points about Charlotte Brontë's portrayal of Jane's story in *Jane Eyre*.
- You write a balanced essay exploring both sides of the argument.
- You use a range of literary terms correctly, e.g. **archetype**, **denouement**, **folklore**, **motif**.
- You write a clear introduction, outlining your thesis, and provide a clear conclusion.
- You signpost and link your ideas.

A02 — Demonstrate detailed critical understanding in analysing the ways in which structure, form and language shape meanings in literary texts.

- You explain the techniques and methods Charlotte Brontë uses to portray Jane and her story, and link them to main themes of the text.
- You may discuss, for example, the way that Jane's story seems to echo the fairy-tale 'Cinderella', as she moves from a position somewhere between servant and young lady to that of romantic heroine who overcomes a number of obstacles and finally marries the hero; or the dialogue between Rochester and Jane, which is evocative of their growing relationship and typical of a type often found in love stories.
- You explain in detail how your examples affect meaning, e.g. Jane's sense of social isolation and obscurity is used to great effect by the author, who makes Jane an acute observer of the world around her on the reader's behalf. But her role as first person **narrator** also makes us less aware of how unusual Jane is, and of other characters' responses to her and their perception of her relationship with Rochester.
- You may explore how other aspects, such as the setting – the house of Thornfield, its garden and grounds – are involved in the portrayal of Jane, and the question of whether her story is a love story.

A03 — Explore connections and comparisons between different literary texts, informed by interpretations of other readers.

- You make relevant links between *Jane Eyre* and other novels with similar themes.
- When appropriate, you compare the portrayal of the heroine in *Jane Eyre* with that of other novels, e.g. images of coming of age in *The Magic Toyshop*.
- You incorporate and comment on critics' views of *Jane Eyre* and its status as a romance.
- You assert your own independent view clearly.

A04 — Demonstrate understanding of the significance and influence of the contexts in which literary texts are written and received.

You explain how relevant aspects of the social, literary and historical contexts of *Jane Eyre* are significant when examining the main thrust of Jane's story. For example, you may discuss:
- Literary context: Jane takes on a role from fairy tale, but her fate reflects an irresolvable clash between romance and **Realism**.
- Historical context: Jane's progress is connected to the legal and economic position of women with respect to property, education and marriage law in the 1840s.
- Social context: Jane's choices are limited by Victorian society's highly gendered understandings of respectability and social class.

* This mark scheme gives you a broad indication of attainment, but check the specific mark scheme for your paper/task to ensure you know what to focus on.